VALENTINE INFANTRY TANK
VS
PANZER III

North Africa 1941–43

BRUCE OLIVER NEWSOME, Ph.D.

OSPREY PUBLISHING

Bloomsbury Publishing Plc

Kemp House, Chawley Park, Cumnor Hill, Oxford OX2 9PH, UK

29 Earlsfort Terrace, Dublin 2, Ireland

1385 Broadway, 5th Floor, New York, NY 10018, USA

E-mail: info@ospreypublishing.com

www.ospreypublishing.com

OSPREY is a trademark of Osprey Publishing Ltd

First published in Great Britain in 2023

© Osprey Publishing Ltd, 2023

A catalogue record for this book is available from the British Library.

ISBN: PB 9781472857279; eBook 9781472857293; ePDF 9781472857286; XML 9781472857309

23 24 25 26 27   10 9 8 7 6 5 4 3 2 1

Maps by Bounford.com

Index by Angela Hall

Typeset by PDQ Digital Media Solutions, Bungay, UK

Printed and bound in India by Replika Press Private Ltd.

Osprey Publishing supports the Woodland Trust, the UK's leading woodland conservation charity.

Artist's note

To find out more about our authors and books visit **www.ospreypublishing.com**. Here you will find extracts, author interviews, details of forthcoming events and the option to sign up for our newsletter.

Abbreviations

RACTM   Royal Armoured Corps Tank Museum, Bovington

Panzer *Ausführungen*/variants are referred to throughout this work in abbreviated form, e.g. 3L – Panzer III Ausf. L etc.

A note on measure

Both Imperial and metric measurements have been used in this book. A conversion table is provided below:

1in. = 2.54cm

1ft = 0.3m

1yd = 0.9m

1 mile = 1.6km

1lb = 0.45kg

1 long ton = 1.02 metric tonnes

1mm = 0.039in.

1cm= 0.39in.

1m = 1.09yd

1km = 0.62 miles

1kg = 2.2lb

1 metric tonne = 0.98 long tons

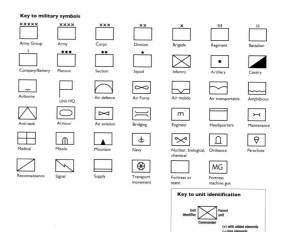

Front cover, above: A Valentine III in action in the desert. (Adam Hook)

Front cover, below: A Panzer III Ausf. L firing. (Adam Hook)

Title page photograph: A Valentine XI serving in North-West Europe as the command tank for a battalion of M10 tank destroyers. (RACTM 0081/C/4)

CONTENTS

INTRODUCTION

The Panzer III and the Valentine tank were designed to meet operational requirements during the arms race that preceded the outbreak of World War II. By the middle of the war, they were the preponderant tanks on the German and British frontlines respectively. With the exception of the Panzer IV, the Panzer III was Nazi Germany's longest serving and most produced tank platform of the war, accounting for about one-quarter of the tanks produced in Greater Germany and Czechoslovakia. Likewise, the Valentine was Britain's and Canada's longest serving and most produced tank platform of the war, accounting for (with its derivatives) about one-quarter of all the tank platforms produced in Britain, about one-quarter of those produced in Canada, and almost three-quarters of the tanks exported by both Britain and Canada to the Soviet Union.

The Panzer III and Valentine were equivalent in many qualitative aspects. Their initial main guns were almost of the same size. The Panzer III received longer and larger guns during the same period, but belatedly the Valentine caught up in terms of lethality. Conversely, although the Valentine started with thicker armour, improvements to the Panzer III meant that the German tank soon made up for the initial deficit in protection.

In terms of operational service, the Panzer III fought in Poland in 1939, Western Europe in 1940, Eastern Europe from 1941, North Africa from 1941 and Italy from 1943. The two tanks' service overlapped most in North Africa, where the Valentine fought from mid-1941 to mid-1943. Valentine variants continued to serve in Italy through the end of the war. Valentine XI command tanks served from late 1944 in North-West Europe. Some Panzer IIIs, despite the preponderance of later types of German tanks, continued to serve in Italy and France from 1943 through 1944, while others were still serving with neglected garrisons in Scandinavia and the Balkans at the end of the war. Valentine tanks continued in Soviet service in Eastern Europe, in Australian and New Zealand service in the South Pacific, and in British service in India and Burma, through the end of the war.

The Panzer III and Valentine fought each other most intensively in North Africa, from November 1941 to May 1943. At times, each was the predominant type on their respective sides. Throughout the entire period, the most numerous German tank type in North Africa was the Panzer III. The Valentine was the second most predominant British tank type (behind the Crusader) in Libya and Egypt by 1942. The availability of the Valentine increased given its uniquely high volume of production (true in both Britain and Canada) and its exceptional reliability amongst Allied tanks. British dependence on the Valentine in the field increased as a result of the Ministry of Supply's failure to upgrade the Matilda II, which was retired from frontline service in August 1942, and the ongoing remediation (since 1941) of the Churchill, the fourth and final infantry tank ever to be deployed. Consequently, the Valentine was the predominant British tank type in Tunisia from November 1942 to March 1943, as British tank formations switched from British to US tanks.

Panzer IIIs and Valentines first fought each other in Libya, during Operation *Crusader* (18 November–30 December 1941), when Panzer 3Es led the counter-attacks against Valentine IIs. They fought almost constantly as Axis forces advanced from Libya into Egypt, from January to August 1942. Valentine IIs sought to recapture Ruweisat Ridge in the Western Egyptian desert on 22 July 1942 in the largest concentration of Valentines yet, only to be almost wiped out by towed artillery and about 20 counter-attacking Panzer 3Js and earlier types. They fought again when Axis forces launched their offensive against the Allied line at El Alamein in Egypt on 30 August 1942, and during the British Eighth Army's counter-offensives of September and October. On 23 October 1942, Valentine IIs led the assaults during the final Allied offensive from the Alamein Line. In subsequent weeks, Valentine IIs led assaults

The Panzer 3E was assembled from December 1938 with a 37mm main gun. (RACTM 2354/A/3)

that liberated Egypt and carried the Allies into Libya in November, while the dwindling number of Panzer 3Js still led the counter-attacks.

The high point of the duel between Panzer IIIs and Valentines was on 1 December 1942, the midpoint of the war, in faraway Tunisia. More Valentines than any other British tank type had landed during the British First Army's invasion of Tunisia in November 1942. Valentine IIIs were deployed for the first time, with three men in the turret (as in all the Panzer III turrets), enabling faster operations than were possible from the Valentine II's two-man turret.

The Germans were quick to respond. The nascent 190th Panzer Battalion, followed by a battalion from the reforming 10th Panzer Division, were sent from France, with mostly Panzer 3Js and 3Ls. Moreover, Panzer 3Ns fought for the first time, each armed with a short 75mm gun, in support to a few Tiger tanks, which arrived with the first of the nascent Heavy Panzer battalions (501st). Thus, the latest marks of the preponderant tank platforms on the British and German sides were set for a duel that would decide the fate of Tunisia.

The Panzers were organized for the first German counter-offensive in Tunisia, on 1 December 1942. Would the Allies keep hold of Tebourba and advance down the few dozen miles of highway to Tunis, thus completing their conquest of Tunisia before winter set in? Would the Germans drive the Allies out of Tebourba, stabilize the front until summer 1943, and delay any Allied invasion of Italy until too late in the summer to be decisive?

The opposing tanks were the latest in their respective series and more closely matched, with some interesting asymmetries. The long 50mm guns on the Panzer 3Js and 3Ls were larger than the 40mm guns on the Valentines. The short 75mm gun on the Panzer 3Ns was most effective as a close-support weapon. The Panzer 3J's armour was not as thick as the Valentine's, but was face-hardened. The Panzer 3Ls and 3Ns were built with thicker armour. However, the Valentine was smaller and stealthier. The Panzer IIIs were more powerful and faster, but the Valentines were lighter, longer in range, and better at crossing obstacles. Which tank would triumph?

CHRONOLOGY

1934
January German Army authorities specify the eventual Panzer III.
April British Army authorities specify the first Infantry Tank.

1935
Trials of bids to parent the Panzer III.

1936
Daimler-Benz wins bid to lead the Panzer III programme.
September British try the first infantry tank (Matilda).

1937
April Panzer 3A delivered.

1938
January Panzer 3D delivered.
February War Office invites Vickers to develop the third infantry tank.
March War Office rejects Vickers' first mock-up Valentine.

1939
April War Office invites Vickers back to design the Valentine.
September Germany invades Poland; Britain declares war on Germany.

1940
May Valentine I delivered; Germany invades France and the Low Countries.
September Valentine I lands in Canada.

1941
May First Valentine VI delivered.
June First Valentine IIs despatched to Egypt for operations; Axis forces invade Soviet Union.

November Valentines first go into action (in Libya).

1942
May Fifteen Valentine IIs join invasion of Madagascar.
July First Axis offensive on Alamein Line.
October Final Allied offensive from Alamein Line.
November Valentines land in Algiers and advance into Tunisia.
December German counter-offensive at Tebourba, northern Tunisia.

1943
March British First Army withdraws Valentines; British Eighth Army uses Valentine IXs for first time, in offensive against Mareth Line, southern Tunisia.
May End of campaign in North Africa.
June British Army withdraws Valentines from expeditionary forces in Europe.
August Production of Panzer III ends.

1944
May Production of Valentine ends.
June Allies invade Normandy.

1945
May Germany surrenders.

This Panzer 3G was knocked out in Libya, in the winter of 1941–42.
(RACTM 18-A-5)

DESIGN AND DEVELOPMENT

REQUIREMENTS

In January 1934, the German Army specified two classes of tank: a light-medium type (eventually the Panzer III) would mount a high-velocity main gun to destroy enemy tanks; a heavy-medium type (Panzer IV) would mount a low-velocity gun/howitzer to fire high-explosive at artillery and infantry behind cover. The Panzer III was intended to be the most numerous tank type. Indeed, it would fulfil that role until 1943. In July 1934, however, the German Army specified the Panzer II as a stopgap pending availability of the Panzer III.

In April 1934, the British Army identified a requirement for three classes of tank: a light tank for reconnaissance and fast pursuit operations; a cruiser tank for exploitation of breakthroughs (largely independent of other arms); and an infantry tank for direct support of pedestrian infantry in the assault, in order to break through fortified defences in particular.

In January 1936, the War Office ordered from Vickers a pilot vehicle of what was designed effectively as a thickly armoured light tank, accommodating just two men and one machine gun (project code A11; eventually named Matilda). This was delivered in September 1936.

These Panzer 3Gs were assembled in 1940, up-armoured, and shipped to Libya in early 1941. (RACTM 142/A/1)

A side shot of a Valentine I and a Matilda II, on a Warflat wagon, illustrating the Valentine's lower profile and simpler production, but inferior armour protection and cramped interior. (RACTM 0062/G/3)

The pilot vehicle convinced the War Office of the need for a medium-weight infantry tank mounting a 40mm 2-pdr anti-tank gun (project A12; eventually named Matilda II). The War Office's own design authorities developed the Matilda II from their own A7E3 experimental medium tank, before passing the project to the Vulcan Foundry.

In April 1937, the Vulcan Foundry refused the Mechanization Board's invitation to develop another medium tank at the same time as the Matilda II. On 10 February 1938, the War Office, desperate for more medium tanks, invited Vickers to develop a derivative of the Vulcan Foundry's Matilda II or Vickers' heavy cruiser (A10; Cruiser II). Vickers naturally chose to develop the latter.

This Panzer 3G was disabled during an attack on Tobruk on 1 or 2 May 1941. (RACTM 163/B/2)

Delays in the production of Cruisers and Matildas exacerbated the War Office's desperation for a stopgap infantry tank. Matilda Is were issued to British Army units from summer 1938, but Vickers continued to be slow with its deliveries, focusing instead on the development and production of other armaments. The Vulcan Foundry too felt under-compensated and was distracted by more profitable opportunities. The result was that the Matilda II did not enter mass production until September 1939.

This Valentine I illustrates the wide internal mantlet common to the Valentine I, II, IV, VI and VII. This tank has the first design of track, with malleable cast iron shoes and the double pin links. (RACTM 1787/A/4)

SPECIFICATIONS

The German specifications of January 1934 included an armour standard of 15mm (0.6in; equivalent to that of a British light cruiser tank), a speed of 40km/h (25mph), and a bridging weight limitation of 24 metric tonnes (23.6 long tons). The immediate dispute was over armament. The German Army wanted a 50mm gun, but the Ordnance Department (Waffenamt) settled for a 37mm gun, in common with the infantry's towed anti-tank carriage. The Ordnance Department promised that the turret would be large enough to allow upgrading to 50mm guns.

The promise regarding turret size was enabled by a separate specification common to the Panzer III and Panzer IV: space in the turret for a commander, a gunner and a loader. A driver and a machine-gunner sat side by side in the front part of the hull. This five-man crew would not be matched by the first three types of British infantry tank: the Matilda accommodated just two crewmen; the Matilda II was specified with three in the turret, but no hull machine-gunner; and the Valentine accommodated only a commander, a gunner and a driver. The Panzer III was most ergonomic and the easiest of the two tank types to up-gun, but the Valentine was the smaller and the lighter design.

On 10 February 1938, Vickers told the War Office that the capacity of the A10 platform was 16 long tons. The company calculated that it could meet the minimum armour standard (60mm) but not the specification for a three-man turret. Instead, in an effort to free up some space in the turret, the company suggested a Vickers 40mm cannon in place of the specified Royal Ordnance 40mm 2-pdr gun.

As inducements, Vickers promised that the automotive line would need no development, and promised production from March 1939. The company also estimated a production cost about two-thirds of the Matilda II. The price of production in the first contract of 1939 would actually be about nine-tenths that of the Matilda II. Accepting these promises, the War Office agreed to a mock-up tank with a 50mm armour basis and a Vickers 40mm cannon – but it would soon realize its mistake during the design and development phase.

PANZER 3L OF 2ND COMPANY, 2ND BATTALION, 7TH PANZER REGIMENT, 10TH PANZER DIVISION, 1 DECEMBER 1942

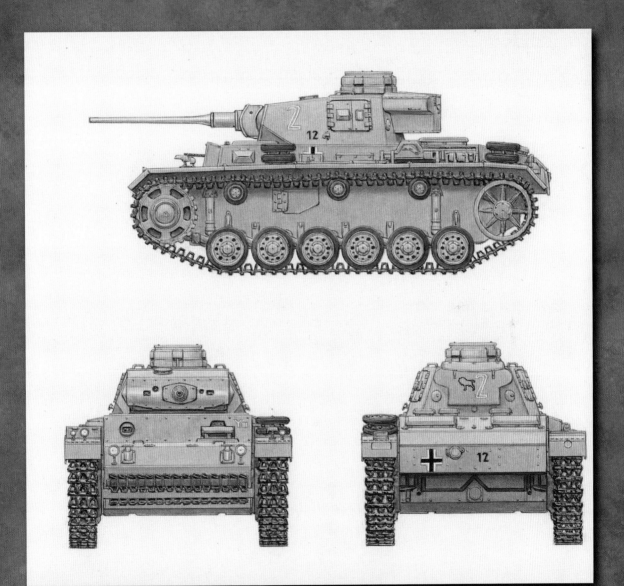

TABLE 1: Panzer III design features by mark

Panzer III Mark	Evolutionary basis	External differentiation						Internal differentiation		
		Main armament	Coaxial MG	Turret front	Turret sides	Turret rear	Hull	Fighting compartment	Radio	Engine compartment
A	Revolutionary			15mm armour			5 roadwheels and coil springs; 2 return rollers; 15mm all around			HL108TR engine; manual 5-speed gearbox
B	A			8 roadwheels, on 2 bogies, each with a large horizontal leaf spring; 3 return rollers						
C	B			8 roadwheels, on 4 bogies, each with a horizontal leaf spring						
D	C	37mm L46.5 KwK36	Two MG 34s	30mm armour			Leaf springs now angled; five vision slits added			6-speed synchromesh gearbox by Aphon
E	D			Improved ventilator in roof			6 roadwheels, each sprung on a transverse torsion bar; 30mm armour front and sides	3 crewmen; manual-only traverse	Fu.2 receiver plus (in platoon and company HQ tanks) a Fu.5 transmitter-receiver	HL120TR engine; 10-speed gearbox with pre-selector by Maybach
F	E	400th vehicle mounted 50mm L42 KwK38	400th vehicle mounted one MG34 instead of two	Internal 30mm mantlet switched to 50mm external mantlet with 50mm L42 gun	30mm	30mm; stowage box on some vehicles	5 smoke generators on tail			HL120TRM engine
G	F	Most as per Panzer 3F; a few as per Panzer 3E		Cupola vision slits are closed by pincer-type shutters, instead of sliding shutters			5 smoke generators on tail			HL120TRM engine

		Armament	Turret	Hull	Crew/traverse	Radio	Transmission
H	G	50mm L42 KwK38	Lower, thicker cupola (50–95mm armour)	Extra 30mm plates bolted to front and rear; 400mm wide tracks, instead of 360mm; idler with 8 spokes, sprocket with 6 apertures instead of 8 circular holes, although older types in stock were used up with spacers; wider spaced return rollers			Improved 6-speed synchromesh gearbox by Aphon
J	H	Later vehicles mounted 50mm L60 KwK39 / One MG 34	50mm at front; 20mm spaced plate on later products / 30mm; gunner's vision slits deleted from 50mm L60 turret / 30mm	50mm at front; modified driver's visor and machine-gun mounting	3 crewmen; manual-only traverse	Fu.2 receiver plus [in platoon and company HQ tanks] a Fu.5 transmitter-receiver	
L	J	50mm L60 KwK39	20mm spaced plate on mantlet	20mm spaced plate on front			
M	L		No vision slits in sides; taller, self-sealing exhaust, allows wading to 1.5 metres (5 feet)				
K	M	First command version to retain main armament	Large port in place of coaxial machine-gun aperture			Fu.2 and Fu.6 (battalion HQ) or Fu.6 and Fu.8 (regimental HQ)	
N	M	75mm L24 KwK37	No 20mm spaced plate on mantlet			As Panzer 3A	

The Panzer 3J with short 50mm gun was assembled from March 1941, just after the German intervention in Libya, where this example was captured. (RACTM 2896/D/6)

DESIGN AND DEVELOPMENT

In 1935, the German Army's Ordnance Department ordered pilot vehicles from Daimler-Benz, Krupp, MAN and Rheinmetall. Daimler-Benz won the bid in 1936, although development was more than a couple of years away from mass production.

The first five *Ausführungen* (marks or models) were really developmental. Deliveries started in April 1937, of what was designated Panzerkampfwagen III Ausführung A (henceforth: Panzer 3A). Ausf A through E were characterized by major variations in the running gear; five road wheels and five coils each side (Panzer 3A); eight road wheels and two leaf springs (3B); and eight road wheels and four leaf springs (3C). The improved load distribution encouraged a doubling of the armour standard to 30mm (Panzer 3D, January 1938). The transmission too was upgraded, from a manual five-speed gearbox to a six-speed with a pre-selector. The Panzer 3E (December 1938) was the final developmental mark, with three remarkable changes that would serve all subsequent marks: torsion-bar suspension for each of six road wheels, each side; a new engine, generating 300bhp (224kW) instead of 250bhp (186kW), by which the vehicle finally reached its specified speed; and a ten-speed gearbox.

Meanwhile, on 24 March 1938, between the first Panzer 3D and 3E, Vickers showed a mock-up Infantry Tank Mark III or Valentine. User and mechanization authorities refused the 50mm armour standard and the commander's means of vision (limited to a single periscope), and reasserted the 2-pdr gun by Royal Ordnance. For a while, the project was dormant.

By April 1939, Panzer 3E production was at its peak, but mass production of the Matilda II was delayed yet again. The War Office invited Vickers back. The company offered a choice between a three-man turret with a 50mm armour standard, or a two-man turret meeting the 60mm armour standard. The War Office opted for the latter.

VALENTINE III OF 2ND TROOP, A SQUADRON, 17TH/21ST LANCERS, BLADE FORCE, 1 DECEMBER 1942

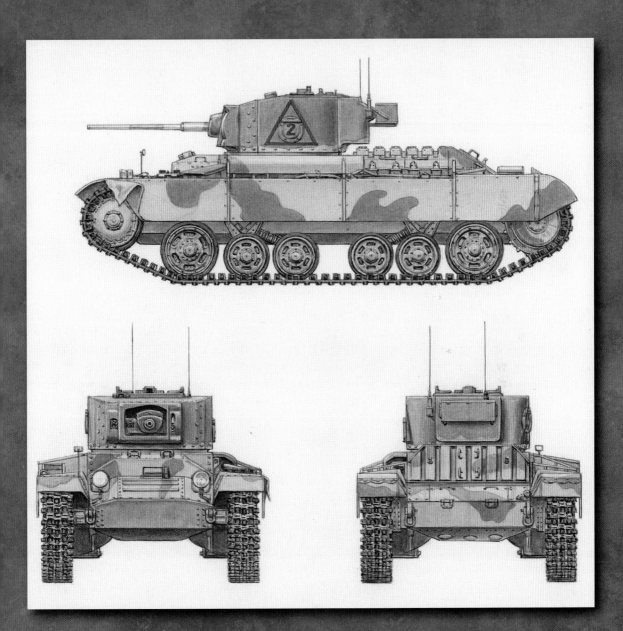

TABLE 2: Valentine design features by mark

Valentine Mark	Evolutionary basis	External differentiation					Internal differentiation			
		Main armament	Coaxial machine gun	Turret front	Turret sides	Turret rear	Hull	Crewmen in fighting compartment	Radio	Engine compartment
I	A10 (Cruiser II)			Internal mantlet, behind a wide rectangular curved opening	On right side: square revolver port. On left side: either no port or a D-shaped port (mostly Valentine IIs)	Armoured cover hanging down over the air exfiltration slit; earlier design ended with a straight edge; most covers had a curved lip; Army workshops would add bracketed boxes on each corner (each for 2 Bren magazines)	All riveted and bolted; 100 Valentine Is had hinges and handles on only the nearside rear access door, and a fuel tank filler under a flap towards the offside; 75 Valentine Is had hinges and handles on both doors, and fuel filler on inside	2	Number 11 low power with 6-foot rod aerial	AEC spark-ignition engine, with fuel tanks either side, Meadows gearbox
II	Valentine I with AEC diesel engine	40mm 2-pdr gun without muzzle brake or counter-weight	7.92mm Besa on right side of main armament					2	Number 11 or Number 19	AEC diesel engine with fuel tank on nearside, Meadows gearbox
III	Valentine II with three-man turret			Internal mantlet, behind an almost square flat mounting; narrow elliptical casting at base of main gun	Circular revolver ports on both sides	Commander's rotating hatch set towards rear; bulge slopes backward and downward towards straight edge; one large box for Bren magazines bracketed centrally and horizontally	As final Valentine Is; Desert Service vehicles had sand guards, auxiliary fuel tank on left track guard, and container for 5 water cans below the access doors	3	Number 19	
IV	Valentine I with GMC engine			As Valentine I/II	As Valentine I/II	As Valentine I/II, except all had curved exfiltration cover		2		GMC 6.71S diesel, Spicer gearbox
V	Valentine IV hull; Valentine III turret			As Valentine III	As Valentine V	As Valentine III		3		

16

Mark	Description	Main armament	Machine gun	Mantlet	Hull / port	Additional	General	Production	Engine
VI	Valentine IV adapted to Canadian industrial capacity	40mm 2-pdr gun without muzzle brake or counter-weight	7.62mm Browning from sixteenth vehicle onwards	As Valentine I/II, except after first 100 vehicles the rivets were eliminated, although still bolted around the top and bottom	As Valentine I/II, except D-shaped port added after first 100 vehicles		As Valentine I/II, except cast nose after first 100 vehicles; otherwise riveted and bolted; splash angles in front of turret ring	Number 11	GMC 6.71S diesel, Spicer gearbox
VII	Valentine VI adapted to No. 19 radio					As Valentine IV, except first vehicle had straight exfiltration cover			
VIIA	Valentine IV with changes to exterior and engine compartment		7.62mm Browning				As above, with: protective cages over headlamps; convoy lamp; ice-studs on tracks; auxiliary fuel tank		As above, except: extra engine oil cooler; batteries moved to rear
VIII	Valentine III with 57mm gun	57mm 6-pdr gun, with counter-weight on muzzle [Mark III was shorter than Mark V]		External mantlet			As Valentine III		AEC diesel
IX	Valentine V with Valentine VIII's turret		None	External mantlet; Mounting Number 1 Mark 1	Circular revolver ports on both sides; backwards-sloped bracket for two 4-inch smoke projectors on right side		As Valentine V	Number 19	540 vehicles had GMC 6.71S; 783 vehicles had GMC 6.71A
X	Valentine IX with Besa machine gun		7.92mm Besa in protruding box on right side of main armament	External mantlet; Mounting Number 4 Mark 1		As Valentine III, except box is bracketed at a slope; Vickers welded all these tanks, but Metropolitan Cammell welded only the last Valentine XIs	As Valentine IX, except: mostly welded, some rivets; protective cages over headlamps; splash angles in front of turret ring		
XI	Valentine X with 75mm gun	75mm gun with muzzle brake (one hole each side)		External mantlet; Mounting Number 1 Mark 5			As Valentine X, except cast nose		GMC 6.71A diesel

2

PRODUCTION

Production of the Panzer III ran from April 1937 and reached its target of 108 deliveries per month in November 1940, at a time when only about 200 Panzers of all types were being produced. Eight firms assembled Panzer IIIs, twice as many as ever assembled Valentines in both Britain and Canada. In total, 6,094 Panzer IIIs (excluding non-turreted variants) were assembled, all in Germany, from April 1937 to August 1943, when all remaining assemblers switched to the assault-gun variant (Sturmgeschütz or StuG III).

A Panzer 3E or 3F being loaded on a wagon at the factory in 1939. (RACTM 163/4/2)

TABLE 3: Production of Panzer IIIs, by type

Type	Total new assemblies
Panzer 3A	10
Panzer 3B	10
Panzer 3C	15
Panzer 3D	30
Panzer 3D Command	30
Panzer 3E	96
Panzer 3E Command	45
Panzer 3F	450
Panzer 3G	594
Panzer 3H	286
Panzer 3H Command	175
Panzer III J	1,521
Panzer III J Command	81
Panzer 3L	1,470
Panzer 3M	517
Panzer 3K Command	50
Panzer Flamm	100
Panzer 3N	614
TOTAL	**6,094**

Valentine production was slower to start, although ultimately greater in numbers. In April 1939, Vickers had estimated full production from April 1940, at four tanks per month. On 15 May, Vickers was told to produce 50 Valentines per month, while Metropolitan-Cammell Carriage & Wagon – a Vickers subsidiary – and Birmingham Railway Carriage & Wagon Company (BRCWC), both of which specialized in the production of rolling stock, were told to produce 125 Valentines per month. No pilot vehicles were ordered.

In July 1939, an order was placed with Vickers for 275 Valentines to be delivered in May 1940. That same month, Vickers delivered a Valentine I for trials, which proved satisfactory, at which point it was recorded as a delivery (12 June). Metro-Cammell and BRCWC delivered one Valentine I each for inspection in July 1940.

In early September 1940, a British detachment landed in Canada with a Valentine I and a Matilda II. The Matilda II shortly travelled on to the United States, while the Valentine I stayed at Camp Borden, home of the Canadian Tank School. The Ministry of Supply's tank mission ordered the Angus Works of the Canadian Pacific Railway Company in Montreal (a subsidiary of the American Locomotive Company) to assemble 300 Valentine hulls. The British mission ordered British-designed armaments and ammunition from suppliers on the other side of the St Lawrence River, but sourced the General Motors Corporation (GMC) Type 6004 two-stroke, six-cylinder diesel engine, the Spicer five-speed gearbox, and suspension arms from the United States.

Meanwhile, British home authorities and contractors redesigned the Valentine II as the Valentine IV to accommodate the US-sourced sub-assemblies. Late in 1940, they despatched a Valentine IV pilot vehicle with a set of technical drawings, which the Canadians then redrew for metric units and locally sourced armour. L.E. 'Ted' Carr was despatched from the British Tank Mission in the United States to help, resulting in a cast nose being adopted after the first 100 vehicles. The Canadian version was designated the Valentine VI, until the turret was redesigned slightly to accept a No. 19 wireless set, resulting in the Valentine VII. The Valentine

This Valentine II illustrates the distinctive engine compartment of all Valentines: air was taken in over the engine and expelled by fans through the sloping rear. The armour covering the air exfiltration slit at the rear of the turret has a curved lip; earlier covers had a straight lip.
(RACTM 0083/G/4)

These Valentine VIs and a US M3 light tank are in Soviet use.
(RACTM 5544/C/3)

The Valentine III received a larger turret for three crewmen, with a narrower aperture in front of the internal mantlet. (RACTM 0076-A3)

VIIA was adapted slightly for Soviet use. The first Valentine VI was paraded for the press at Angus Works on 27 May 1941.

The Canadians delivered 73 Valentines in 1941. The British had delivered about 350 by the end of 1940, and delivered about 1,000 more in 1941, while the Canadians delivered 943. Vickers production peaked in December 1942 at 81 Valentines for the month, declined most rapidly at the end of 1943, and ended in May 1944, when production switched to the Archer 17-pdr self-propelled anti-tank gun.

From May 1940 to May 1944, 7,260 Valentine tanks (5,840 British, 1,420 Canadian) excluding variants were produced, of which 3,782 were exported to the Soviet Union (2,394 British; 1,388 Canadian, of which only 3,332 arrived). Two Canadian tanks were retained by Britain. Thus, effectively, 3,782 Valentine turreted tanks were assembled on Soviet account, 3,448 on British account, 30 on Canadian account.

TABLE 4: Production of Valentine tanks, by type	
Type	Total new assemblies
Valentine I	308
Valentine II	1,511
Valentine III	536
Valentine IV	524
Valentine V	996
Valentine V DD	212
Valentine VI	30
Valentine VII	1,390
Valentine VIII	0
Valentine IX	1,087
Valentine IX DD	236
Valentine X	135
Valentine XI	120
Valentine XI DD	175
TOTAL	**7,260**

DEPLOYMENT

Valentine production eventually surpassed that of the Panzer III, but while most Panzer III designs went into action, most Valentine designs did not. In 1940 and 1941, the War Office allocated Valentines to British Army armoured divisions, pending the arrival of cruiser tanks. Their use as infantry tanks remained questionable: the Matilda II was better protected; and the Infantry Tank Mark IV (later known as the Churchill) was in development with even thicker armour. Furthermore, both were assembled with side skirts over the running gear; both accommodated three men in their turrets; and both were more mobile across country than the Valentine. However, the Valentine was the easiest of the three to transport, its automotive line was more mature and thus promised to be the most reliable, and it was the smallest in profile and lightest in weight.

Repeatedly, from November 1940 through June 1941, the Director of Armoured Fighting Vehicles (DAFV), Major-General Vyvyan V. Pope, recorded Valentines as stopgaps, and denied their suitability as infantry tanks, mostly because of inferior armour protection, particularly the lack of side skirts to protect the running gear.

At that time, almost all Valentines were being used as stopgap cruisers in three of the five armoured divisions at home. As of 1 June 1941, 902 were in service, of which only four were overseas (for trials or demonstrations).

In June 1941, following a request from Middle East Command for more cruiser tanks, Pope allowed for Valentines to be sent overseas as stopgap cruisers. However, the first 50 Valentine IIs enshipped as infantry tanks to replace the Matilda IIs of 8th Battalion Royal Tank Regiment (RTR) that had been sunk in transit the previous month. The Valentines were not used in action until Operation *Crusader* commenced on 18 November.

First Army Tank Brigade's other two battalions (42nd and 44th RTR) were equipped with Matilda IIs until they were replaced by Valentines during 1942. The 7th RTR was converting from Matildas to Valentines when captured at Tobruk in Libya on 21 June 1942. A Special Service tank squadron (about 15 Valentines) was used during the invasion of Madagascar in May 1942.

On exercise in England in 1941, these Valentine Is or IIs have the curved lip over the air exfiltration slit at the rear of the turret, and the centrally located bulbous base for the 6ft rod aerial used with the No. 11 wireless radio. The No. 19 wireless set was used with a shorter, thinner aerial on the offside of the turret roof for higher echelon traffic, and an even shorter aerial on the nearside for traffic within the troop. (RACTM 4477/F/2)

The Panzer 3J with longer 50mm gun was assembled from December 1941, and served in Libya soon thereafter. (RACTM 0163-H2)

By 21 June 1942, 660 Valentines had been shipped to Egypt, although perhaps half had been knocked out or captured. On 22 July, the newly landed 23rd Armoured Brigade lost almost all of its 100 Valentine IIs in an attack on Ruweisat Ridge largely without other arms. For the offensive from El Alamein (23 October 1942), Eighth Army held 223 Valentines, of which 169 were employed by 23rd Armoured Brigade, which had grown from two battalions to four, each of which supported an infantry division as doctrinally prescribed. As of 7 November, 23rd Armoured Brigade had lost 171 tanks (19 completely destroyed, 55 awaiting recovery, 29 in third-line workshops, 68 already repaired and returned). This brigade was withdrawn from the frontline (until 23 February 1943).

In autumn 1942, Valentine IIIs (three-man turrets) were issued to squadron and troop commanders. On 13 November 1942, 6th Armoured Division landed through the port of Algiers with Valentine IIs, Valentine IIIs, Crusader II close-support tanks (76mm howitzers) and Crusader IIIs (57mm 6-pdr guns). However, they would be faced by Panzer III Js and 3Ls with long 50mm L60 guns, and Panzer 3Ns with short 75mm guns operating in close support to Tiger tanks. While the Valentines were expected to lead a quick conquest of Tunisia, the Panzer IIIs were ordered to throw the Allies out of the country, starting with the first German counter-offensive on 1 December 1942.

TABLE 5: Numbers of Panzer IIIs and Valentines with formations on or near the front at the start of key campaigns and battles in the West, 1939–44

Date	Operation	Panzer IIIs	All Panzers	Panzer IIIs as % of all Panzers	Valentines	All Allied tanks	Valentines as % of all Allied tanks
1 September 1939	German invasion of Poland	c.120 (37mm)	c.2,400	5	-	-	-
10 May 1940	German invasion of France	388 (349 with 37mm; 39 command)	2,574	15	-	-	-
31 March 1941	German intervention in Libya	64 (60 with 50mm; 4 command)	154	39	-	-	-
6 April 1941	German invasion of Greece	74 (27 with 37mm; 44 with 50mm; 3 command)	142	52	-	-	-

18 November 1941	Allied Operation *Crusader*	140 (136 with 50mm; c.4 command)	253	55	c.52 (Valentine II)	759	7
1 July 1942	First Axis offensive on Alamein Line	c.40 (c.15 with 50mm L42; 25 with 50mm L60)	c.55	73	c.50	179	28
22 July 1942	Allied attack on Ruweisat Ridge, Egypt	c.20	c.25	80	100	106	94
30 August 1942	Second Axis offensive on Alamein Line	172 (93 with 50mm L42; 73 with 50mm L50; 6 command)	238	69	c.100 (Valentine II)	c.590	17
23 October 1942	Final Allied offensive from Alamein Line	173 (85 with 50mm L42 and command; 88 with 50mm L60)	242	71	169 (Valentine II)	1,050	16
1 December 1942	German counter-offensive, Tebourba, Tunisia	c.40 (34 with 50mm; 4 with 75mm; 2 command)	68	59	25 (Valentine II and III)	217	12
14 February 1943	Axis counter-offensive, central Tunisia	149 (130 with 50mm; 19 with 75mm)	c.206	72	c.100 (Valentine II and III)	c.480	21
20 March 1943	Allied offensive on Mareth Line, southern Tunisia	c.53	c.84	63	c.80 (Valentine II, III and IX)	c.450	18
22 April 1943	British-French offensive, Goubellat Plain, Tunisia	c.63	c.99	62	40 (Valentine II and III in French use)	733	5
6 May 1943	Final Allied offensive in Tunisia	c.32	c.52	62	45 (Valentine II and III in French use)	1,136	4
10 July 1943	Allied invasion of Sicily	63 (49 with 50mm L60; 3 with 75mm; 11 command)	158	40	-	-	-
June to August 1944	Normandy, France	30	1,720	2	-	-	-

Source: Bruce O. Newsome, *The Rise and Fall of Western Tanks*, Volume II: *1939–1945* (Tank Archives Press, 2021).

THE STRATEGIC SITUATION

On 23 October 1942, the British Eighth Army launched its final offensive from the Alamein Line in Egypt. The Italian-German Panzer Army in Africa (Generalfeldmarschall Erwin E. Rommel) was greatly disadvantaged materially. Within days it was in retreat into Libya, while planning a final defensive line inside French Tunisia – about 1,250 miles to the west.

These Panzer 3Gs are advancing in Yugoslavia in April 1941. (RACTM 0243-A3)

On 8 November 1942, American, British and Free French forces invaded the main ports of Morocco and Algeria. Most of the French and colonial defenders surrendered or switched sides within days.

ALLIED PLANS

The Eastern Task Force landed in Algiers on 8 November, while the Western Task Force and the Central Task Force landed in Marrakesh (Morocco) and Oran (Algeria) respectively. The advance into Tunisia did not start until 10 November. The tanks did not land until 13 November.

Tunisia is a huge and challenging area of operations, being 500 miles from north to south

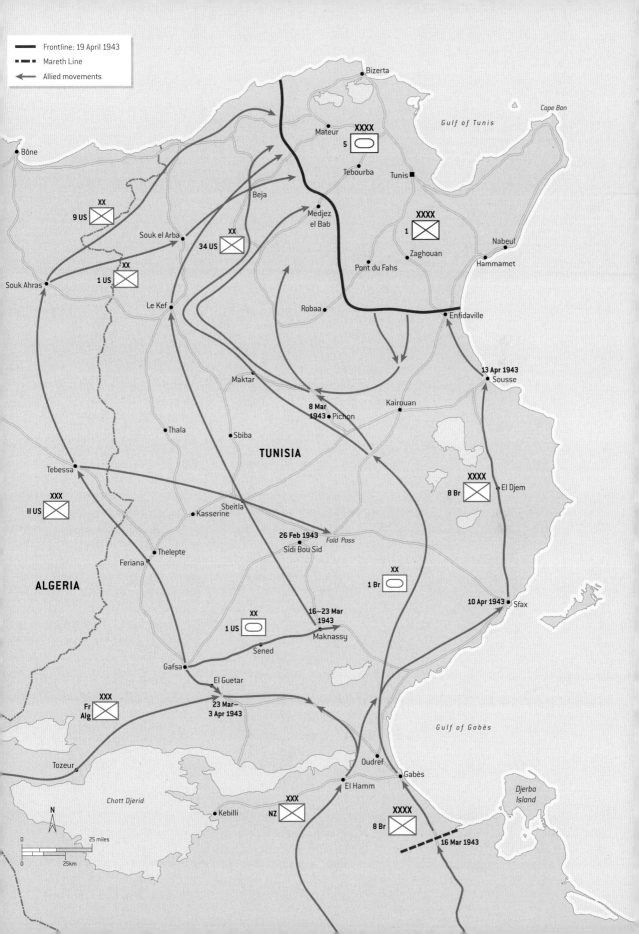

Frontline: 19 April 1943
Mareth Line
Allied movements

Bône

Bizerta

Cape Bon

Gulf of Tunis

Mateur

5 XXXX

Teboudba

Tunis

9 US XX

Souk el Arba

Beja

Medjez el Bab

34 US XX

1 XXXX

Nabeul

Zaghouan

Hammamet

Souk Ahras

1 US XX

Le Kef

Pont du Fahs

Robaa

Enfidaville

13 Apr 1943 Sousse

Maktar

8 Mar 1943 Pichon

Kairouan

TUNISIA

Thala

Sbiba

8 Br XXXX

El Djem

Tebessa

Sbeitla

II US XXX

Kasserine

26 Feb 1943
Sidi Bou Sid

Faïd Pass

1 Br XX

Thelepte

10 Apr 1943 Sfax

Feriana

ALGERIA

1 US XX

16–23 Mar 1943

Sened

Maknassy

Gafsa

Fr Alg XXX

El Guetar

23 Mar–
3 Apr 1943

Gulf of Gabès

Tozeur

Oudref

Gabès

El Hamm

Djerba Island

Chott Djerid

Kebilli

NZ XXX

8 Br XXXX

16 Mar 1943

N

0   25 miles

0   25km

This Valentine I or II is with 20th Armoured Brigade, 6th Armoured Division (whose symbol is the mailed fist painted on the nose), in Britain, during summer 1941. (RACMT 1789/E/6)

and 150 miles from east to west, with mountains and muddy plains in the north and rocky deserts in the south. The distances, terrain, multi-national suspicions and poor interoperability help to explain but not excuse Allied failures. Allied leaders and commanders exacerbated the natural difficulties with a series of poor choices. The Americans chose to secure the territories closer to neutral Spain than Axis Europe, even though the British, up to Prime Minister Winston S. Churchill, predicted no Spanish hostility. The Allies estimated it would be at least two months before German forces could fight their way through Spain or force Spain to take action, and forecasted only 'token resistance' from the French. Yet Allied decision-makers insisted on landing outside the range of Axis aerial predominance, and within range of Allied fighters based at Gibraltar.

GENERAL DWIGHT D. EISENHOWER

Dwight David 'Ike' Eisenhower (1890–1969) graduated from the US Military Academy at West Point in 1915 with no remarkable academic or professional focus. His first appointments were nominally with the infantry, but practically administrative. In 1918, incongruously, he was given command of a nascent tank battalion, which never left the United States. He subsequently specialized as a trainer, policy researcher, adviser and planner, serving a series of influential generals, including ultimately the Army's Chief of Staff, General George C. Marshall.

In June 1942, Eisenhower took over the European Theatre of Operations HQ (based in London), which became Allied Forces Headquarters (AFHQ) for expeditions in the Mediterranean Rim. Eisenhower moved to Gibraltar on 5 November, flew to Algiers on the 13th, and based himself there on the 23rd, after the first 'dash' had failed. He spent most of his North African period touring French political authorities in Morocco and Algeria. His staff remained split between London, Gibraltar, Algiers and Marrakesh.

LIEUTENANT-GENERAL KENNETH A.N. ANDERSON

Kenneth Arthur Noel Anderson (1891–1959) was commissioned into the Seaforth Highlanders in 1911. He served in France from 1914 to 1916, and Palestine in 1918. He was back in France from 1939 to 1940, in command of an infantry brigade. His subsequent commands were in Britain, until he led the inexperienced First Army to Algeria in 1942. US Army Brigadier General Paul M. Robinett (commander of 13th Armored Regiment and deputy commander of Combat Command B, 1st Armored Division) passed through Anderson's Advanced HQ on 27 November:

> He expressed the opinion that we would soon end the campaign in Tunisia. But General Anderson impressed me as something of a juggler, playing with three balls representing Tunis, Bizerte, and Tunis-Bizerte, who could not decide whether to concentrate on one or the other or try for them both at the same time. His personality and manner were good, but he seemed something of a dreamer. After talking with him, however, I felt very keenly that though he had the responsibility at the front, he had nothing to say about affairs at the rear. He would have to get along with available means, not being able to order additional resources to the front. Nothing was said to indicate such a state of affairs, but I sensed the fact, nevertheless.

Allied commanders were confident, but their intelligence and plans were vague. General Dwight D. Eisenhower (Commanding General, European Theatre of Operations), his deputy (Major General Mark W. Clark), and the commander of the Western Tank Force (Major General George S. Patton) did not attend the final planning conference in Britain. No mention was made of Axis intervention in Tunisia.

The Eastern Task Force was allowed to land no closer to Tunisia than Bone, more than 63 miles by road from the border. From Bone, Blade Force was ordered to dash to Tunis (about 175 miles by the shortest available route) to forestall German intervention, even though its Valentine and Crusader tanks were very different in terms of speed.

This Valentine II is configured for Desert Service with auxiliary fuel tank, sand guards over the tracks, and a container for five water cans on the rear; it has not yet been finished in sand-coloured paint. The tracks are of the third type, with more links and single pins, for more reliability. (RACTM 0076/A/4)

This Valentine II is being demonstrated in Egypt in early 1942. (RACTM 5730/C/5)

Once Blade Force was ashore, higher commanders procrastinated while waiting for regional politics to settle and for ground personnel to establish air bases. Another excuse was the shortage of infantry in case of urban fighting (Tunis alone accommodated 220,000 residents).

AXIS PLANS

The Axis held no forces in Tunisia before the Allied invasion, and thus had no plans. Nevertheless, they started landing airborne and naval infantry from 9 November, and planned a counter-offensive.

On 13 November, the regional commander (Generalfeldmarschall Albert Kesselring, in Rome) told Generalleutnant Walther K. Nehring (commander of the newly activated German XC Corps) that the situation was 'difficult and urgent' and that he should try to thrust westwards as far as the Algerian frontier 'in order to gain freedom of movement'. On 14 November, Nehring landed in Tunis to gather information. He was intent on sending airborne troops in available vehicles as a delaying force the next day.

The terrain was difficult enough for the Allies even when they did not face resistance. It would be more difficult for the German counter-offensive, now that the Allies had occupied Tebourba and the approaches from Djedeida and Mateur. The soil

This Befehlspanzer III (command tank) is in Yugoslavia in April 1941. The fake main armament and extra aerials are characteristic of command tanks until the Panzer 3K.
(Bundesarchiv, Bild 101I-185-0137-14A/Grimm, Arthur/ CC-BY-SA 3.0)

This Panzer 3K Befehlspanzer command tank – featuring all the armament and armour of the Panzer 3M, plus extra ports and radios – was photographed by the Soviets in January 1944. (RACTM 2355/D/6)

was predominantly yellow clay, as in most of northern Tunisia, which becomes impassable to even the best tracked vehicles after rain (Americans described its consistency as being like chewing gum). Rain was the predominant weather in the winter months. Tebourba, which normally accommodated 4,000 residents, most of whom had evacuated, is contained within a loop of the Medjerda River, olive groves, cork woods and scrubby, rocky hills.

Nehring planned his counter-offensive through the most open terrain, to the north and north-west of Tebourba. Axis forces could reach this rolling plain by several routes from Mateur. However, the highway had been blocked, at the hilly pass near the village of Chouigui, since 25 November, by the US element of Blade Force.

GENERALLEUTNANT WALTHER K. NEHRING

Walther Kurt Nehring (1892–1983) joined an infantry regiment in 1911. He commanded the 18th Panzer Division during the invasion of the Soviet Union in 1941, then the *Deutsches Afrikakorps* from May 1942 until being wounded on 31 August 1942. He was flown out of North Africa on 10 September and was still being treated for a festering wound to his arm on 9 November, when he was consulted about the situations in Egypt and Tunisia. He left Berlin on 11 November, on orders to take command of a new defensive line to the rear of the line broken near El Alamein in Egypt, but on 12 November, while in Rome, he was ordered to Tunisia. Generalfeldmarschall Albert Kesselring briefed him the next day. Nehring left on 14 November, in Kesselring's plane, intent on a brief overview of the situation in Tunis before returning the same night. After a flight of 75 minutes, the plane crashed on landing and was written off (although nobody was hurt). At that time, no chief of staff was available for the corps; the highest staff officer was the chief of operations (Major Josef Moll), who was on the same flight, along with a major detailed by Kesselring to handle 'matters pertaining to the command of ground forces'. Nehring brought a personal assistant (Leutnant Sell). After flying back to Rome to report, Nehring, Moll and Sell were soon back in Tunis. A major arrived later as adjutant, followed by a leutnant as assistant to Moll.

TECHNICAL SPECIFICATIONS

ENGINES

All the powerplants used in Panzer IIIs were V12 spark-ignition engines. The Panzer 3A to 3D mounted an HL108TR engine produced by Maybach, developing 250bhp (186kW). From the Panzer 3E (December 1938) onwards, the standard engine was the HL120TR, developing 300bhp (224kW) at 3,000rpm. From the Panzer 3F, the engine was modified slightly under the designation HL120TRM. Panzer IIIs allocated for tropical or North African service (the Panzer 3G (Tp) onwards) were assembled or retrofitted with a faster cooling fan and additional air filters.

All the powerplants in the Valentines were small six-cylinder in-line engines, although the Valentine was lighter than the Panzer III. The Valentine I, as delivered from May 1940, had an A189 spark-ignition engine produced by AEC, developing 135bhp (101kW). The Valentine I never left Britain, however, due to the unreliability of this engine.

The Valentine II and III received the slightly less powerful but more economical A190 diesel version. AEC was already an unreliable supplier, however, so, early in 1940, the Ministry of Supply's Directorate of Mechanization (from July 1940 the Department of Tank Design or DTD) evaluated a GMC diesel engine of the same power. The Valentine IV was a Valentine II adapted for the GMC engine and a Spicer gearbox. All Valentine IV–VIIs and 540 of the 1,323 Valentine IXs received the GMC 6.71S engine (the 'S' type of the Type 6004 engine). The 'A' type (with larger fuel injectors and a higher governed speed) developed 165bhp (123kW) and went into 783 Valentine IXs, all Valentine Xs and all Valentine XIs.

GEARBOXES

The Panzer 3A was given a five-speed manual gearbox, the Panzer 3D a ZF-made Aphson SSG 76 six-speed synchromesh gearbox, the Panzer 3E a ten-speed Maybach Variorex gearbox with semi-automatic pre-selector, and the Panzer 3H an Aphson SSG 77 six-speed manual gearbox. The Variorex's seventh to tenth gears provided marginal advantage for greater unreliability. This had been mitigated initially by governing the speed to 40km/h (25mph).

These Panzer 3Hs are entering Thessaloniki, northern Greece, in April 1941. (RACTM 2356/E/1)

The Valentine I, II and III had a five-speed clash-type gearbox made by Meadows. The Spicer gearbox (Valentine IV, May 1941, onwards) had clash gears in first and fifth, and synchromesh gears in second, third and fourth.

TRACKS

Panzer III tracks, which started at 360mm wide, were increased to 400mm from the Panzer 3H (October 1940) onwards. The wheels were widened commensurately. The opportunity was taken to introduce simplified idler and drive wheels (differentiated by their apparent spokes), and to even out the spacing of the return rollers, although legacy wheels were used with spacers on early Panzer 3Hs.

The Valentine's tracks became progressively more durable but heavier. They started with cast iron track shoes with double pin links, but within months more durable steel shoes were substituted. The third and final type of track was developed by the DTD in 1941, with more links and single pins, for more reliability. Most of the track shoes were cast manganese steel, but some were stamped from slightly heavier 30-carbon steel, and are identifiable by slightly rounded ends. All later Valentine IIs and subsequent Valentines, including all Canadian-built examples, were delivered with the third type of track.

ARMOUR

The Panzer III started in 1936 with a maximum armour thickness of just 15mm, but during development the specification increased to 30mm (Panzer 3D turret, January 1938; Panzer 3E all around, December 1938). When up-gunned with the 50mm L42,

Later Panzer 3Js and the Panzer 3L differed from previous models mostly in the spaced armour bolted over the mantlet and the driver's plate. (RACTM 4868/A/3)

the mantlet of the Panzer 3G (April 1940) boasted an armour thickness of 35mm. The Panzer 3H (October 1940) was assembled with duplicate 30mm plates on the front, for a total of 60mm. The Panzer III J (March 1941) was assembled with 50mm face-hardened plates at the front.

The 40mm 2-pdr gun's armour-piercing (AP) shots lacked the tough caps found on German AP shots, and so tended to shatter against face-hardened plates. The British Army Training Memorandum Number 40 (July 1941) clarified that 2-pdr guns, on the defensive, 'must be sited well forward in defiladed positions affording maximum ranges of no more than 800 yards to the target area if German Mark III or IV tanks are likely to be met'. In October, Middle East Command's Training Memorandum Number 2 complained of users' over-optimism, and ordered that 'fire from an AFV with the 2-pounder should not be opened at a greater range than 800–1,000 yards'. In March 1942, in British tests, the fronts of captured Panzer IIIs were proof against 2-pounder shots at all ranges. Gunners were subsequently advised to fire only on the Panzer III's sides and rear, which in theory they should defeat up to 1,500 yards away.

At the time of the Valentine's introduction to service, its armour was thicker than that of any current Panzer III. In November 1941, when the Valentine first fought, the latest German tank type in Libya was the Panzer III J, with 50mm of armour at its thickest. The Valentine's armour standard was 60mm, but some of it was cast, which is softer than the rolled plates, at 65mm. With standard German ammunition – armour-piercing, with a tough cap, a ballistic cap for aerodynamics, and a high-explosive base charge (APCBCHE) – the 37mm L46.5 gun could not perforate the Valentine's front at any range. The 50mm L42 could defeat a Valentine at up to 900 yards away, the 50mm L60 at up to 1,100 yards. With armour-piercing composite rigid (APCR) shots, the L46.5 could defeat the Valentine at up to 400 yards, the L42 and L60 at up to 1,500 yards. With high-explosive anti-tank (HEAT: shaped-charge warhead) shots, the 75mm L24 gun could perforate the Valentine at any range.

The Valentine's armour was never upgraded. By contrast, from September 1939 to June 1942, the Panzer III's maximum armour thickness increased from 30mm (3E) to 35mm (3F), 50mm (3J), 60mm (3H) and 70mm (3L, 3M, 3K, 3N). In the field, however, crews of the Panzer 3L and later tanks sometimes removed the spaced armour from the mantlet to improve the gunner's vision. The Panzer 3M and later tanks were designed to carry side skirts too, 5mm thick beside the hull and 8mm thick around the turret, but these were sometimes carried away by collisions or impacts.

In theory, the 57mm 6-pdr gun's shots could perforate the Panzer 3J and 3H at all practical ranges, although the uncapped shot might still shatter. Capped shot was not routinely available until spring 1943. By then, even capped shot might be defeated in the space between the 20mm outer plate and the 50mm structural plate on the Panzer 3L and later tanks. British tests showed that the penetrative range of 57mm APC shots was reduced from 2,500 yards to 600 yards. The 20mm outer plate was deleted from

the Panzer 3N's mantlet in compensation for the heavier gun, so the mantlet was vulnerable to the 2-pdr at up to 700 yards and the 6-pdr at up to 2,500 yards, if the shot did not shatter. The 6-pdr did not receive armour-piercing discarding sabot (APDS) shots until June 1944, by which time heavier Panzers were predominant.

From 1943, the Valentine's hull side armour was reduced from 60mm to 43mm to compensate for the extra weight of the 6-pdr gun and later the 75mm gun. The side plates were then vulnerable to the 37mm gun at up to 750 yards and the 50mm guns at 1,500 yards with standard shots. On all Valentines, the belly plate inclined to where it met the side plates: this incline helped to deflect blast but could be perforated by projectiles as small as German 7.92mm armour-piercing bullets.

Panzer IIIs were welded from the start, except for the hull and superstructure, which were bolted together. The Valentine's plates were mostly bolted and riveted, which tends to be a weaker form of joining than welding. Vickers did not switch to welding-only until the Valentine VIII. Metropolitan-Cammell did not make the switch until the Valentine XI.

From late 1942, British technicians evaluated captured Panzer 3Js with cracked plates for the first time. The plates' metallurgy was discovered to be inferior, a result of Germany suffering shortages of key alloying elements. These low-toughness plates tended to be used as roofs or bellies, where they were less likely to suffer kinetic impact.

COMBUSTIBILITY

Valentines tended to combust at a greater frequency than the Panzer III, if only because the German guns fired shots with base charges, which none of the Valentines fired until the Valentine XI. Most types of Valentine benefited from the use of diesel fuels, which are less volatile than petrol, although in any case fuel is less hazardous than ammunition. Many fires in Valentines would start in the fighting compartment

These Panzer 3Ls were issued to 1st Company, 502nd Heavy Tank Battalion, in Fallingbostel, Germany, in summer 1942. (RACTM 7368-A3)

due to sympathetic ignition from a perforating shot's base charge, without the fuel ever combusting.

Panzer III ammunition was stowed within boxes made from 5mm (0.20in) armour. The Valentines IX, X and XI were the first British tanks to be assembled with armoured ammunition bins; but each successive mark lost stowage capacity in favour of armament, which was bad for lethality but good for survivability.

The Panzer III's fuel tanks were assembled with 5mm-thick armour plates. One day in May 1941, Leutnant Joachim Schorm of 6th Company, 5th Panzer Regiment, in Libya, heard 'a crash just behind us … The tank must be on fire … I turn around and look through the slit. It is not burning. Our luck is holding.' Later he extracted a shot from the right-hand auxiliary fuel tank, from which the fuel had drained without igniting.

The Valentine's fuel tanks were not armoured. In the event of a fire in the engine compartment, the driver was supposed to press the engine shutdown button (shutting off both fuel injectors and the air), and to turn off the fuel tap near his seat. The commander's position was provided with another button for shutting down the engine. The Valentine had a Pyrene fire extinguisher inside the turret, a second outside. The gunner was closest to the former, with which he could fight an engine fire through the bulkhead door.

OBFUSCATION

The Panzer 3F (September 1939) was fitted with five smoke generators on the tail, which the commander activated via a spring-loaded pull rod – each pull released one candle. Each candle was propelled from the rack by means of a spring, then automatically ignited, and left behind on the ground to produce smoke. The springs were activated by a camshaft, with the cams placed around the shaft at 72 degrees. From later Panzer 3Hs onwards, the rack was concealed under the engine air outlet cowling.

Late Panzer 3Ls and subsequent tanks were fitted with a set of three NbK39 smoke-grenade dischargers on each side of the turret, all six facing forward. The three dischargers in each set were aimed at slightly different angles in order to distribute the 90mm smoke grenades forward in a slight arc.

The Valentine I, II, IV, VI and VII had a 2in mortar for firing smoke, fitted in a separate mounting to the right of the main mounting. During trials, users complained that the breech, when 'broken' for loading, would foul the feed box to the machine gun. A redesigned mortar was incorporated into the Valentine III onwards.

Given the Valentine IX's larger main gun, the 2in mortar was replaced by two 4in

'smoke dischargers' on the right side of the turret, in a fixed mounting, angled to project about 125 yards. In addition, two 'smoke generators' were at the rear, one on each track guard. These were controlled by two buttons on the driver's left-most instrument panel. Whereas the turret dischargers projected the grenades, the generators on the rear caused the grenades to emit smoke without projection.

ARMAMENTS

The Panzer arm had specified a 50mm gun for the Panzer III since 1935, but Ordnance had settled for the 37mm L45 KwK36 (Panzer 3A to early Panzer 3F). From April 1940, Panzer IIIs were delivered or upgraded with the 50mm L42 KwK38 (late Panzer 3F to Panzer 3J). In February 1941, however, Hitler discovered Ordnance's choice of the L42, in defiance of his order to upgrade straight to the 50mm L60. Compliance with his order would take the rest of 1941 to execute.

On 21 April 1941, Middle East Command's first report of a German 50mm tank gun reached London. After examination of captured arms in Tobruk, on 8 May Middle East Command reported that the 50mm gun could penetrate 60mm of armour at up to 400 yards, and damage running gear at up to 2,500 yards.

The Panzer III could stow 120 rounds of 37mm ammunition. Even with 50mm ammunition, it could stow 99 rounds. The Valentine, however, could stow only 79 rounds of 40mm ammunition, because of its much smaller turret. The 2-pdr gun was slightly quicker to fire, but useless against the face-hardened plates on the fronts of Panzer IIIs.

BRITISH 40MM 2-PDR GUN POSITION IN VALENTINE TANK

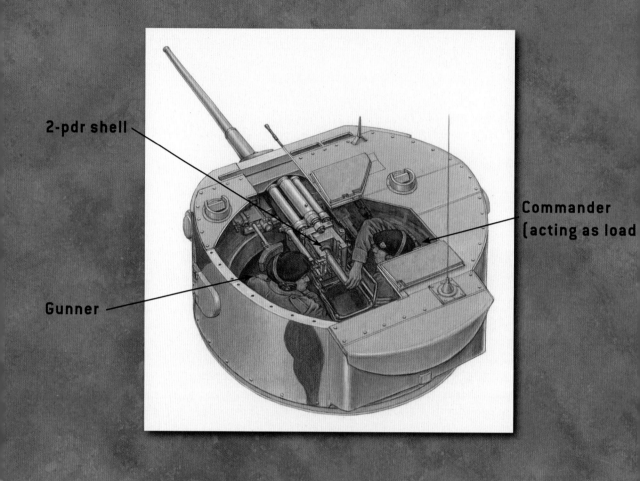

2-pdr shell

Gunner

Commander
(acting as load

In May 1941, the Ministry of Supply took delivery of the first Valentine IIIs – the first member of the Valentine family to be fitted with a three-man turret – at the same time as the Canadians delivered their equivalent, the Valentine V. In September 1941, the General Staff declared the Valentine obsolete, and urged rearmament with the 57mm 6-pdr gun as a stopgap. However, in December 1941, the Ministry of Supply reported that the tank's turret did not offer sufficient room for a larger gun, but promised a self-propelled 6-pdr.

From December 1941, the 50mm L60 KwK39 was mounted in the 400th factory-assembled Panzer 3J and in retrofitted Panzer 3Hs. Nineteen of these were with German units in time for the Axis offensive on 26 May 1942, as the British knew from signals intercepts. The German signals described these tanks with the suffix 'Lang', which the British easily translated as 'long' and connected with the towed L60 they had discovered a year earlier. (They referred to the Panzer III Lang as the 'Mark III Special'.) In British tests, the L60 gun could perforate the Valentine's armour standard

In Tobruk, 20 April 1942, a British Royal Engineer demonstrates to infantry where best to place an explosive charge on a Panzer 3F upgraded with a 50mm L42 gun. (RACTM 6616/A/5)

at up to 300 yards with standard ammunition. US Army Ordnance reported an effective range of just 500 yards and a maximum range of 770 yards with 57mm APCR, and an effective range and a maximum range of 1,000 yards with APCBCHE.

One of the penalties of fitting the longer gun was a reduction in 50mm ammunition stowage, from 99 to 84 rounds in the Panzer 3J, and just 78 rounds in the Panzer 3L (the armour of which was thicker). The mounting of the longer gun in the Panzer 3L and 3M differed mostly in the torsion bar used to spring the gun's equilibrator, in contrast to the compression spring seen in previous Panzers.

On 4 June 1942, Vickers sent to the British Army's mechanical experimental establishment a 6-pdr self-propelled gun on a Valentine I hull for automotive trials, but after just 76 miles it was sent back on 6 June without further interest. Around then, the Ministry of Supply authorized a Valentine with a 6-pdr gun. The DTD accommodated the 6-pdr, but with a two-man turret and no coaxial machine gun. The prospect of combination of this turret and the Valentine II/III hull was known as Valentine VIII. The Valentine V hull was substituted in order to standardize the GMC engine, but with thinner side armour. This combination was the Valentine IX, which was piloted in June 1942 and mass-produced from late 1942.

Also in June 1942, the Panzer 3N was delivered, with the 75mm L24 gun/howitzer, for use as a close-support weapon. The L24 could fire high explosive or smoke against artillery, or a shaped charge against armour. Some Panzer 3Ls were retrofitted with the same weapon.

The 2-pdr and 6-pdr guns still lacked high-explosive or smoke ammunition, so British Army tank squadrons were equipped with two close-support tanks, on one of the Cruiser platforms. In Tunisia, each Valentine-equipped tank squadron also featured two Crusader close-support tanks, and a troop of Crusader IIIs (with 6-pdrs). In February 1943, the New Zealand Army converted 18 Valentine IIIs to close

GERMAN 50MM L60 KWK 39 (KAMPFWAGENKANONE 39)

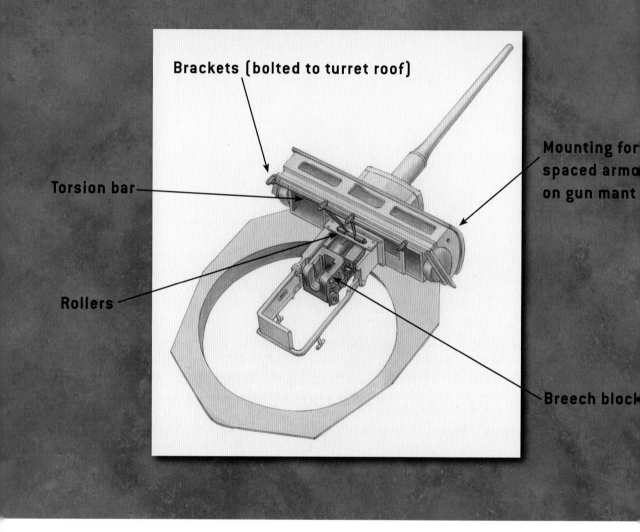

Brackets (bolted to turret roof)

Torsion bar

Mounting for spaced armo on gun mant

Rollers

Breech block

OPPOSITE

Inside a Panzer 3L, the gunner sits to the left of the main gun, with his left hand on either the elevation wheel or the traverse wheel, his right hand on the range dial around the gun sight, and his brow against the pad above, except when he is looking through the visors to his side. (RACTM 6361/E2)

support. The 76mm howitzer was optimized to fire smoke, although some high-explosive rounds were issued, but it never received a shaped-charge round.

By then the British wanted most of its tanks to fire US 75mm ammunition, the high-explosive warhead of which was superior. This would be a late addition to the Valentine series, as the Ministry of Supply was still struggling to meet the required specifications for a 6-pdr-armed Valentine. The Valentine IX reached the front by March 1943, but was resented for its lack of a machine gun (except for a Bren light machine gun in stowage) and the lack of space for a loader. The Valentine X, which was delivered from July 1943, benefited from having a coaxial machine gun, but still no loader. The Valentine XI, which was delivered from February 1944, mounted a 75mm main gun and a coaxial machine gun, but still there was no space for a loader.

TABLE 6: Penetrative performance in British tests of tank guns against rolled homogenous armour set at vertical

Nationality	German	British	German	German	German	German	British
Range (yards)	37mm L46.5 APCBCHE	40mm L53 AP	50mm L42 APCBCHE	50mm L42 APCR	50mm L60 APCBCHE	50mm L60 APCR	57mm L45 AP
100	50	70					106
200	46.5	67					103
400	41	59.5					96
500			68	104	78	120	
600	36.5	52.5					90
700			63	97	73	101	
800	32	48					84
1,000	28	44	58	81	61	84	78
1,200			54	84	57	70	

GUNNERS' POSITIONS

In both the Panzer III and the Valentine, the gunner sits to the left of the main armament, in front of a coaxial sighting telescope. If he is sitting in a Panzer 3J or earlier, he can look through a slit in the front turret or a slit in the side, but these were eliminated from late Panzer 3Js onwards, given the new mounting for the larger 50mm gun.

The Valentine's gunner could utilize a rotating periscope above, or a D-shaped port to the side (known misleadingly as a 'rear-view lookout'). This lookout was missing from most Valentine Is and some Valentine IIs, and was welded shut in the field after word got around that bullets could penetrate the joints.

The Panzer III's turret is traversed and elevated manually by respective handwheels. The Valentine's turret is traversed via electrically or manually operated gears. For electrical control, the operator engages the trigger inside the handle, then twists (pivots) the handle from vertical (clockwise for rightwards, anti-clockwise for leftwards). The powered speed is controlled by the degree to which the control handle is twisted. The 2-pdr gun was elevated via a shoulder rest. The 6-pdr and 75mm guns were elevated via manually operated gears.

VALENTINE GUNSIGHT

The No. 30 and No. 33 gunsights offer a magnification of 1.9, and a scope of 21 degrees. It is scaled up to 1,800 yards for firing 2-pdr AP, and 1,500 yards for firing the machine gun. The etched scale is the only aid to ranging. The gunner would elevate the gun until the horizontal line for the estimated range is aligned with the bottom of the target.

DRIVERS' POSITIONS

The Panzer III's driver sits to the left of the machine-gunner, with a hatch above and a pronounced visor in front. The visor is filled with a block of safety glass. On the Panzer 3G onwards, the visor is closed with a single shutter, instead of the rising and falling pair of shutters on earlier marks. When the visor is closed, the driver may look through a binocular periscope, the two ports of which are directly above the visor. The driver can look to his left through a visor in the side armour. The escape doors in the hull sides, between the tracks, were eliminated from the Panzer 3M onwards in order to speed production and because the new side skirts obscured them anyway. The driver's top hatch is large and easy to escape. (One motivation for the size was to help with access to the transmission.)

PANZER III GUNSIGHT

The Turmzielfernrohr 5e (TZF 5e) offers a magnification of 2.5, and a scope of 25 degrees. It is scaled to 1,500m (1,640 yards) for all types of AP shots, and 3,000m (3,281 yards) for HE shells. The gunner uses his right hand to twist a dial to rotate the hemi-circular scale, which is marked in increments of 200m (219 yards), until his estimated range hits the pointer at top centre. A separate glass plate, etched with the aiming triangles, would move up as he decreases the range, down as he increases it. He then respectively lowers or raises the gun's elevation until the target appears above the aiming triangles. He adjusts the traverse until the target is above the central triangle. The apparent size of the target relative to the triangles helps him to estimate its range.

The driver of a Panzer 3E, 3F or 3G benefits from a pre-selector, which allows him to pre-select the gear before he pushes on a pedal to shift gears. The arrangement takes much less thought and effort than the fully manual controls in the Panzer 3H to 3N and all the Valentines.

The driver grips a lever in each hand, which he pushes forward to add power on that side, and pulls back to brake. A foot pedal serves as a throttle for the engine.

To the front-left of the driver is an electric gyroscopic direction indicator: it is not a compass, but is meant to be aligned with a separate compass. The German instructions are for the tank commander to stand 15m (16.4 yards) behind the tank, observing the alignment of the right track guard with a compass in his hand. This reading is then fed into the device, and set (by locking a knob to the position marked Fest), after which the gyroscope was allowed to rotate for three minutes, before driving.

The Panzer 3L's driver sits with his hands on the steering levers most of the time. The gear-shift lever is to his right, below an instrument panel. The gyroscopic compass is to his front left. Visors are to his front and left. (RACTM 6353/B6)

Once set, the gyroscope would adjust the visible dial according to the attitude of the tank, so that the 12 o'clock position remains oriented with North.

The Valentine's driver sits centrally, with two doors either side, opening up to the sides. Each door is sprung by torsion bars to assist opening and closing. The door is locked in the closed position by a bolt, or retained in the open position by another bolt. The door is supposed to be locked, otherwise the motion of it swinging to and fro would wear out the torsion bars. None of the doors could be opened from the outside.

The driver looks through two periscopes – one looking forward right, one looking forward left – and a rectangular aperture in the front vertical plate, closed by a visor. The right-hand periscope could be rotated freely, but is supposed to be aimed at the rear-view mirror on the right track guard. As a precaution, the periscopes can be remounted back to front to present the armoured backside of the mounting to the enemy.

In all the Valentines, the visor can be swung out to the side, controlled from the inside by a lever. If open, the driver is protected by a 'lookout block' (a Triplex block, behind a bullet-proof shield, with four vision slits). The lookout block is considered an emergency option if the periscopes are damaged and the driver is unable to repair them. In case of damage, the whole lookout block can be lowered by releasing the finger catch underneath. The Triplex block can be removed by releasing a finger catch at the bottom left of the shield. Two spare Triplex blocks are carried beside the driver.

Driving is similar in both the Valentine and the Panzer 3H onwards. The Valentine driver's feet operate the clutch pedal (leftmost), the auxiliary brake pedal (middle) – which is rarely needed – and the accelerator pedal (rightmost). The two levers between his knees act as steering and braking levers, operating on respective sides. The levers start in the 'hard on' or 'parked' position, i.e., pulled back (towards the driver) in order to engage the pawls in the central rack (ratchet). To release the brakes, the driver squeezes together the grips of each lever to withdraw the pawls,

VALENTINE AND PANZER III DRIVERS' POSITIONS

A. Valentine driver's position
B. Panzer III driver's position
C. The gyroscopic compass to left front of Panzer III driver

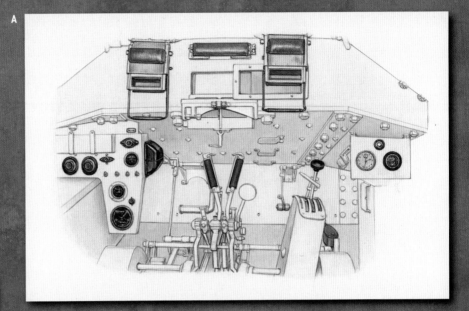

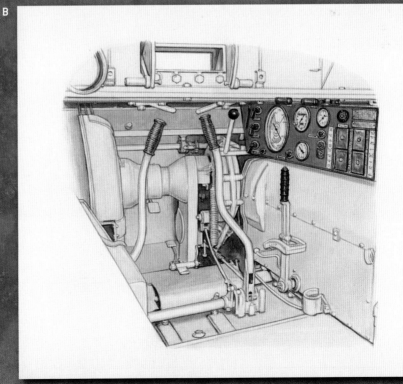

flips over the catch on each lever to hold the grips in the squeezed position, places his thumbs on top of the catches, and pushes the levers fully forward (engaging the clutches in the final drives). When ready to move, the driver depresses the clutch pedal, selects a gear, lets out the clutch, and presses on the accelerator. To steer towards one side, he pulls back the lever on that side. To stop, he pulls back both levers.

The clutch pedal is depressed to release a gear, let out, depressed again to select a gear, and let out again to engage the gear. The gear-change lever is located in a gate on the right side of the driver. The lever is connected by universal couplings, selector rods, and an adjustable actuating lever to the gearbox. The advance normally starts in second gear, with the lever in the middle bottom of the gate. First gear (top-right corner) is provided for uphill or heavy going. The reverse (bottom-right corner) and fifth (top-left corner) gears cannot be engaged until the driver squeezes a catch on the lever.

Forward of the driver, an instrument panel is mounted to the left, a smaller one to the right. The left panel is provided with an ammeter (reading 0 to 60 amps), oil-pressure gauge, speedometer, starter button, an ignition switch for the 'flame primer' for cold-weather starting, a flame primer hand-pump knob, four switches for the exterior lights, a socket for an inspection lamp, and a five-way fuse box.

The commander of this Panzer 3J sits behind the gunner, close enough to gain his attention with his feet. (RACTM 2928/F/2)

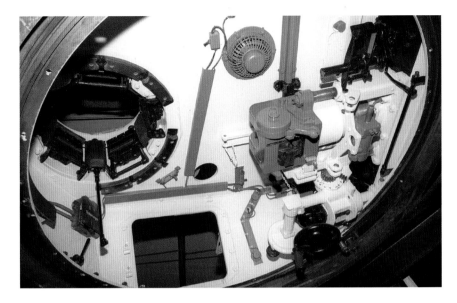

The Panzer III's commander sits with his eyes above the hatch, at one of the periscopes in the cupola, or looking out one of the side hatches or door visors. Here we are looking inside the Tank Museum's Panzer 3L. (RACTM 6353/B2)

On the right panel is a water temperature gauge, an eight-day clock, and the engine shut-down control, which had three definite positions: if fully out, the fuel injectors and air valve were open; if partially depressed, the fuel injectors were closed but the air valve remained open, as a way to stop the engine normally; and if fully depressed, the fuel injectors and air valve were closed, in order to stop the engine in an emergency.

COMMANDERS' POSITIONS

From the start, the Panzer III was assembled with a commander's cupola, cut with five vision slits. These slits are shuttered via mechanical linkages controlled from the inside. The commander can latch them in three positions: open, semi-open and closed. In January 1943, a technical liaison officer reported home from Middle East Command:

> The tank commander's all-round vision from the Panzer III cupola is good. The commander sits in his seat behind the 50 mm gun and just by glancing left, right, ahead, and to the rear, he gets a very good view of the country over a wide range. On the other hand the glasses are apt to become obscured by sand.

The commander can make use of the large hinged double doors in each side of the turret, of which the forward door is cut with a vision slit, and the rearward door is equipped with a pistol port (eliminated from the Panzer 3M onwards). Two pistol ports are in the turret rear.

The Valentine's commander is provided with a hatch, a rotating periscope in the hatch, and a large square 'revolver port' in the right side of the turret. On the roof, in front of the periscope, is a sighting vane.

TABLE 7: Capabilities and performance of Panzer III and Valentine tanks, ordered by date of first pilot vehicle

Year and month of first delivery	Tank name and mark	Lethality					Survivability		Mobility, Tactical				Mobility, Strategic	
		Main gun's barrel calibre [mm]	Main gun's barrel length [calibres]	Main gun's barrel length [mm]	Main gun's volume [cubic mm]	Muzzle velocity [m/s]	Maximum armour thickness [mm]	Height [m]	Engine power-to-weight ratio [bhp/metric tonne]	Speed [km/h]	Nominal ground pressure [kN/m²]	Vertical step [m]	Weight [metric tonnes]	Operating range [km]
1937 April	Panzer 3A	37	46.5	1,720.5	1,849,899	745	15	2.34	16.2	35	67	0.6	15.4	165
1938 January	Panzer 3D	37	46.5	1,720.5	1,849,899	745	30	2.44	12.6	35	92	0.6	19.8	165
1938 December	Panzer 3E	37	46.5	1,720.5	1,849,899	745	30	2.44	15.4	40	92	0.6	19.5	165
1939 September	Panzer 3F	37	46.5	1,720.5	1,849,899	745	30	2.44	15.2	40	92	0.6	19.8	165
1940 April	Panzer 3G	50	42	2,103	4,123,340	685	35	2.44	14.8	40	92	0.6	20.3	165
1940 May	Valentine I	40	50	2,000	2,513,274	853	65	2.27	7.8	24	72	0.8	17.3	164
1940 October	Panzer 3H	50	42	2,103	4,123,340	685	60	2.44	13.8	40	97	0.6	21.8	165
1940 December	Valentine II	40	50	2,000	2,513,274	853	65	2.27	7.6	24	76	0.8	17.3	320
1941 March	Panzer 3J	50	42	2,103	4,123,340	685	50	2.50	7.5	24	76	0.8	21.5	155
1941 May	Valentine III	40	50	2,000	2,513,274	853	65	2.22	7.5	24	76	0.8	17.3	254
1941 May	Valentine IV	40	50	2,000	2,513,274	853	65	2.27	7.5	24	76	0.8	17.3	254
1941 May	Valentine V	40	50	2,000	2,513,274	853	65	2.22	7.5	24	76	0.8	17.3	254
1941 May	Valentine VI	40	50	2,000	2,513,274	853	65	2.27	7.5	40	76	0.8	17.3	254
1941 September	Valentine VII	40	50	2,000	2,513,274	853	65	2.27	7.5	24	76	0.8	17.3	254
1941 December	Panzer 3J Lang	50	60	3,000	5,890,486	835	50	2.50	14	40	97	0.6	21.5	155
1942 June	Panzer 3L	50	60	3,000	5,890,486	835	70	2.50	13.2	40	102	0.6	23.0	155
1942 June	Panzer 3N	75	24	1,800	7,952,156	450	70	2.50	13	40	104	0.6	22.7	155
1942 June	Valentine IX	57	43	2,451	6,254,360	900	65	2.16	7.4	24	78	0.8	17.5	254
1942 October	Panzer 3M	50	60	3,000	5,890,486	835	70	2.50	13.2	40	94	0.6	22.7	155
1943 February	Valentine III CS	76	25	1,900	8,619,274	213	65	2.22	7.5	24	76	0.8	17.3	254
1943 July	Valentine X	57	50	2,850	7,272,512	900	65	2.12	9.4	24	78	0.8	17.5	254
1944 February	Valentine XI	75	36.5	2,737.5	12,093,905	619	65	2.16	9.4	24	78	0.8	17.5	254

Notes: Muzzle velocity is for standard-issue AP rounds, or shaped-charge rounds if AP not issued. See: Bruce O. Newsome, *The Rise and Fall of Western Tanks, Volume II: 1939–1945* [Tank Archives Press, 2021].

PANZER III AND VALENTINE COMPARED

A Panzer 3J with a 50mm L42 gun advances in Libya, April 1941. (Bundesarchiv, Bild 101I-783-0109-11/Dörner/CC-BY-SA 3.0)

In June 1941, the Valentine II was deployed, with comparable lethality (a 40mm gun) to the first Panzer IIIs, thicker armour and a smaller profile. However, the Panzer III got ahead in armament and armour by November 1942. In North Africa, the Panzer III models included the 3F to 3J (with a 50mm L42 gun), the 3J Lang (with a 50mm L60 gun) by May 1942, and the 3N (with a short 75mm gun) by November 1942. By then, the latest Valentine model in service was the Valentine III, the main difference from the Valentine II being a larger turret able to accommodate three crewmen instead of two.

The expeditionary forces in both Britain and the United States were told repeatedly that the latest German tanks were the 'Panzer III Special' (Panzer 3J and 3L, which had reached the front in Egypt by August 1942, with a 50mm L60 gun) and the 'Panzer IV Special' (Panzer 4F2 or 4G with a 75mm L43 gun). This intelligence missed the Panzer 3N and the Panzer VI Tiger, both of which were issued to heavy-tank units, of which one nascent unit would be diverted to meet the Allied invasion of north-west Africa.

Most German tanks encountered in North Africa were Panzer IIIs, but Allied soldiers reported most of them as Panzer IVs. Even the Tigers were reported as Panzer IVs, until correctly identified in January 1943. Panzer IIIs were perpetually underestimated in both quantity and quality, but they still made up the majority of Axis tanks.

THE COMBATANTS

ALLIED FORCES

The Allies formed Eastern Task Force to land in and consolidate Algeria, and simultaneously advance into Tunisia. It boasted the British 1st Parachute Brigade, a US paratroop regiment, two British Army Commandos (1st and 6th), British 78th Division, parts of British 6th Armoured Division, and Combat Command B (CCB) of the US 1st Armored Division.

Once the ports were secure, most of the Allied armoured forces landed from 13 November. The overland invasion of Tunisia comprised two British infantry brigade groups (BGs) with US armoured attachments; and a British-US armoured group (Blade Force). Blade Force was the most tank-dense group and was supposed to operate over the greatest area and at the greatest speed, and to take the lead in striking for Tunis. Blade Force formed with:

- US 1st Battalion (54 M3 light tanks) of 1st Armored Regiment
- 17th/21st Lancers (33 Valentine IIs and IIIs; 18 Crusader IIIs; 6 Crusader II close-support tanks)
- B Squadron of the Derbyshire Yeomanry (10 armoured cars and 10 scout cars)
- B Company of the 10th Battalion of the Rifle Brigade
- A Troop of 5th Field Squadron Royal Engineers (RE)
- C Battery of 12th Royal Horse Artillery (eight 25-pdrs)
- A Battery of 72nd Anti-Tank Regiment (eight 6-pdrs)
- G Troop of 51st Light Anti-Aircraft Regiment (40mm cannons)
- a detachment from 9th Tank Transporter Company
- a transport platoon (Royal Army Service Corps and Ordnance Corps)

COLONEL RICHARD HULL, 17TH/21ST LANCERS AND BLADE FORCE

Richard Amyatt Hull (1907–89) was commissioned into the 17th/21st Lancers in 1926. He served mostly in Egypt and India until 1939, when he returned to Britain. He took command of the regiment in summer 1942, but was away on mixed staff duties from June until mid-September, by which time the regiment was preparing for embarkation. After embarkation, Hull was promoted to full Colonel and commander of Blade Force. Hull lagged behind Blade Force until the eve of the Axis counter-offensive. He was in Souk El Arba, 62 miles west of Medjez by the road via Beja, from 19–23 November. His HQ moved to Beja on 24 November. The next day, it moved to Sidi Nsir, still 23 miles west of Chouigui. Early on 30 November, it moved to a few miles short of both Chouigui and Tebourba. Within 24 hours, the Axis counter-offensive would catch his HQ unawares. No unit recorded any visit from Hull.

- a section from 26th Armoured Brigade's Provost Company
- two sections from 165th Light Field Ambulance

By 1 December, 253,213 Allied troops had landed in Morocco and Algeria. Most never moved on to Tunisia; the result of exaggerated fears of a French rebellion or an Axis invasion through Spain and Spanish Morocco. Nevertheless, the Allied force in Tunisia was larger than the Axis force. Allied records for the forces on the Tunisia front are scant, but they must have held more than 30,000 men, excluding the many garrisons and transitional troops on the lines of communications.

MAJOR-GENERAL VYVYAN EVELEGH, 78TH DIVISION

Vyvyan Evelegh (1898–1958) was commissioned into the Duke of Cornwall's Light Infantry in 1917. His battalion deployed to France and Italy before the end of World War I. He was with the Allied mission to Archangel in Northern Russia in 1919, when he was wounded. His subsequent peacetime years were characterized by staff work. At the start of World War II, he was appointed to the staff of II Corps of the British Expeditionary Force to France. Since this was commanded by Lieutenant-General Alan Brooke, who shortly took command of Home Forces and was promoted to Chief of the Imperial General Staff, Evelegh's wartime career was assured. He commanded 11th Brigade in 1941, and 78th Division from June 1942.

On 29 November 1942, Evelegh told the principals of CCB that everything was going well and he hoped to take both Tunis and Bizerte soon. He worried about the local preponderance of Axis aircraft, however, and so assigned CCB to capture the Axis airfields around Tunis after dark on 1 December. Brigadier General Robinett was not impressed:

Evelegh was an enormous man whose ruddy face was generally animated with a smile. In America, he would have been an ideal selection for Santa Claus, so it was only natural for the men to dub him that behind his back. Evelegh's explanation of the situation and the disposition of his troops was vague. Long after the war, I learned the facts and was amazed at the shotgun fashion in which he had scattered his command in quest of the Germans, who concentrated their meagre forces on vital terrain features.

The British journalist Philip Jordan had written on 26 November: 'The more I see of Evelegh the more I like him. He is a jovial, over-optimistic fellow with a pleasant stutter.' On the 29th, he wrote: 'We are still held up, but Evelegh says he is going to put his armour into Tunis tomorrow. I doubt his ability to do so.'

By then, five Allied brigade groups (excluding French) were in Tunisia: the British 1st Parachute, 11th (with US tanks and other arms) and 36th (with US tanks and other arms); the British-US Blade Force; and the US CCB. Blade Force was officially described as a 'regimental group', but at one point counted a ration strength of 12,000 men. The CCB contributed another 4,000.

Under the terms of the French-German armistice of 1940, the French Armies of Tunisia, Algeria and Morocco were allowed 15,000, 50,000 and 55,000 troops respectively, of which 3,000 were killed or wounded during the invasion. About 9,000 held Medjez. Bizerte held an undecided naval garrison of 14,000, until 12,000 were disarmed by Axis troops on 9 December.

By 1 December, Allied formations in Tunisia held 217 tanks, excluding another 40 on the road. The Germans had landed 68 Panzers in Tunisia, of which they committed about 45 to their counter-offensive that day, including about 40 Panzer IIIs with 50mm guns. On the other side, 25 Valentine IIs and IIIs were ready.

AXIS FORCES

As of 8 November, the Axis had no forces in French Africa, except observers and attachés. The highest Axis authorities had discounted the chance of Allied landings in formally neutral territories. For about a week from 9 November, the Axis arrivals in Tunis were airborne or naval infantry. Their only vehicles were purchased locally. As of 17 November, the Western Allies estimated 500 to 1,000 Axis troops in Tunis, plus 4,000 in Bizerte.

Allied intelligence had estimated that the Germans could move only 10,000 low-grade troops into Tunisia within two weeks of the invasion. As of 30 November,

First Army HQ estimated 15,500 enemy combatants. By the end of November, the Axis had transported 28,187 troops to Tunisia, mostly service, support, replacement and light troops.

The new XC Corps HQ (Generalleutnant Walther K. Nehring) took command of:

- an incomplete German paratroop regiment (two battalions, under Oberstleutnant Walter Koch, in the mountains north of Tebourba)
- a battalion of parachute engineers (outskirts of Mateur)
- a few replacement battalions (*Marschbataillonen*)
- most of the Italian 1st 'Superga' Division, including a battalion of 35 light self-propelled guns (initially at Mateur, later south-east of Tunis)
- a couple of Italian naval infantry battalions (in Bizerte)
- twenty 88mm anti-aircraft guns, of which at least four were advanced as anti-tank guns
- two companies of German armoured cars (scouting far to the south)
- the nascent 190th Panzer Battalion (operating out of Bizerte and Mateur)
- most of 1st Panzer Battalion, 7th Panzer Regiment, 10th Panzer Division
- an infantry battalion, a motorcycle battalion, an anti-tank battalion and an artillery battalion from 10th Panzer Division
- the 501st Heavy Tank Battalion HQ and a few Panzer IIIs and Tigers from its nascent 1st Company, all attached to the 10th Panzer Division

About 64 Panzers were in country, of which 45 (about 40 were Panzer IIIs) were allocated to the counter-offensive on 1 December. Fourteen armoured cars were available. Adding 16 self-propelled anti-tank guns (probably all Marder IIIs) gave a total of 75 German AFVs.

The 1st Panzer Battalion was incomplete, so was made up with elements of the 190th Panzer Battalion. In any case, the attack was not organized in one battalion, but in three *Kampfgruppen* (battle groups): two from the north, and one from the east, the latter of which was out of sight from the other two. Three Tigers and four Panzer IIIs (likely all Panzer 3Ns) from the 501st Heavy Tank Battalion were ready that day. These seven Panzers were the only tanks allocated to the eastern *Kampfgruppe*.

MAJOR HANS-GEORG LÜDER, 501ST HEAVY TANK BATTALION

Hans-Georg Lüder (1908–89) joined the cavalry in 1927, and transferred to the Panzer arm in 1935. In May 1942, he was given command of the new 501st Heavy Tank Battalion. By August, it was allocated to enship to Egypt, but would be diverted to Tunisia. The 501st Heavy Tank Battalion started to entrain its few available Tigers and Panzer IIIs on 11 November; they were enshipped from Italy on the 23rd. Most of the personnel flew to Tunisia. Lüder and his ordnance officer (Generalmajor Wilhelm Hartmann) flew into Tunis on 22 November, where they were tasked to form a *Kampfgruppe*. This commenced its first attack on 25 November. Meanwhile, Hauptmann Nikolai Baron von Nolde (1st Company) commanded the nascent unit.

The Valentine X had a coaxial machine gun on the offside of the 6-pdr gun. (RACTM 1787/A/1)

TRAINING

German Army training changed remarkably little from its first intervention in North Africa until the end, thanks to excellent foundations and Allied difficulties in adapting during a period of rapid expansion and unstable command.

The German Army's *Guidelines for Commanding and Employing the Tank Regiment and Tank Battalion in Combat* (January 1941) prescribe that the regiment's light platoon (five Panzer IIs) should screen ahead, looking for enemy minefields and opportune routes of attack. The light platoon could be supplemented by the light platoon from the nearest battalion, and platoons from the light companies. In Tunisia, each of the 10th Panzer Division's two Panzer battalions held three light companies (17 Panzer IIIs each, including a Befehlspanzer III) and one medium company (12 Panzer IVs and a Befehlspanzer III), although by 1 December 1942 the division had landed slightly fewer Panzers than needed for three companies.

In the attack, one battalion would lead, while the other prepared to develop the first battalion's break in:

> Within each battalion, one Panzer III company should lead, the Panzer IV company should provide fire support from behind, and the other Panzer III companies should bring up the rear, usually in column, but perhaps echeloned towards any exposed flank. In close terrain, Panzer III and Panzer IV platoons may be attached to each other.
>
> By default, a company advances with two platoons in line, followed by one platoon in the centre, the company HQ, and the final platoon. In any case, the emphasis is on depth not width: the attack formation must not be wider than 1,200 metres (1,312 yards).
>
> Self-propelled anti-tank guns should follow closely to take positions on the flanks, in case of enemy counter-attack. Medium companies should reinforce the likeliest position. Most of the light companies should be reserved until the enemy attacks, and should be directed into the attacker's flanks. Enemy tanks must be the first targets. Tanks in flight must be pursued and cut off. Once Panzers break contact, they should look for opportunities to ambush any pursuers. (*Guidelines for Commanding and Employing the Tank Regiment and Tank Battalion in Combat*)

Middle East Command was late to get its first training memoranda out (September 1941). This explicitly sought to learn from the Germans. Its strongest emphasis was on 'combined arms'. Its training memoranda were emphasized in Home Forces, given that it was the most active combatant command from autumn 1940 to 1943. Its training pamphlet for issue to infantry and tank units shipping from Britain is

dated September 1942, but was printed in London in time to arrive in Egypt by August. The pamphlet described itself as the 'common doctrine and technique in the handling of infantry divisions and army tanks in the Middle East'. The first page declared that 'infantry, army tanks, medium guns, anti-tank guns, field and medium artillery, and engineers are all tactically complementary … All arms are therefore dependent on each other, and the closest cooperation between them in every phase of the battle is absolutely essential.' Tanks and infantry were supposed to train together in marching and consolidating the objective, although in practice the units never routinized this.

Across more than 70 pages and eight diagrams, *Training Memorandum Number 1* prescribes a 'combined attack' by infantry and tanks – up to an infantry division with an army tank brigade in support, down to an infantry platoon with a tank troop in support. The scenarios included a practised breach of minefields ahead of a fortified line, a planned attack on an enemy position protected by anti-tank guns, and a hasty attack on an enemy position unprotected by anti-tank guns. The planning guidance includes a 'preparatory period', an 'approach march', an 'assault', and an 'exploitation, consolidation and pursuit' phase.

In the assault, the infantry tanks and pedestrian infantry should advance together:

> The time lag between the arrival of the tanks and infantry on the objective must be reduced to an absolute minimum. To achieve this, the infantry taking part should be divided into three echelons, each with its own quota of anti-tank guns, mortars, and medium machine guns, if available. The leading echelon will follow the tanks straight to the objective which they will clear and consolidate, by-passing any enemy centres of resistance still holding out. The second echelon will protect the flanks by establishing themselves on each side of the penetration and exploiting outwards. The third echelon will mop up the area between the front edge of the enemy's defensive organization and the objective within the flanks of the penetrations.

In November 1942, Middle East Command started putting together lessons from Eighth Army's offensive from the Alamein Line into Libya. These would not be published until January, but they were communicated between principals by letters and lectures. Middle East Command's highest authority for AFVs reported:

> The tank can no longer lead in the attack and put a grateful infantry on to conquered ground. Rather must the infantryman with massed artillery support first gain the objective. Then follows the sapper to clear a passage for supportive arms. The tank's main role at this stage is to arrive betimes to protect the infantry against counter-attack on the ground won. This process must be repeated and a channel be cut right through the defended zones before the armour can begin to pass through to its more spectacular but less strenuous function of cutting communications and blocking withdrawal. Even this role is far more certainly performed with the help of accompanying infantry and artillery. There is still however liable to be a critical period while our armour is making its final exit if the enemy has retained a large part of his own armour and anti-tank guns intact.

He added that 'success depends on the use of all arms in the closest cooperation when the task is to break through an enemy defended area. Such cooperation can only be achieved by the most detailed planning, training, and rehearsal of all arms together.' Cooperation comes from all arms living and training together, as proven by the 23rd Armoured Brigade (Valentine tanks) and the infantry divisions of XXX Corps.

The commander of 23rd Armoured Brigade (Brigadier George W. Richards) wrote this prescription for combined arms assault:

> [Infantry] Brigade and Tank Battalion IOs [intelligence officers] must live with their opposite numbers in the infantry during the period of preparation. By this means they will get to know the ground and the enemy disposition intimately. They will thus be in a position to guide and point out rapidly to the Squadron, Troop and Crew commanders all points which they are required to know, as well as supplying them with sketch maps and panoramas of the ground over which the attack is to take place. Brigade and Battalion IOs will also make a point of contacting artillery OPs [observation posts] who are often in a position to pin-point enemy anti-tank, field gun and machine-gun positions, which are, of course, most useful pieces of information for the tank leaders ... Every officer and NCO must make personal contact with his opposite number in the other arms. It is only by this means that a proper understanding and confidence will be obtained in the battle.

TACTICS

On 28 September 1942, the 17th/21st Lancers were briefed by their new commander, Richard A. Hull, using a cloth model: he foresaw opportunistic, long-distance operations against a scattered, poorly armed enemy, across open country, except for a few mountains. His memorable metaphor was 'hitting a pin with a hammer'. On 1 November, aboard ship, he briefed officers of the 17th/21st Lancers; but the rest of Blade Force, distributed over several ships, heard nothing of this until after landing in mid-November. The higher orders were unsealed aboard ship on 5 November, but these covered only the assault landings.

Once ashore, Hull imparted great confidence but little strategy: he ordered a 'tank-infested area', centred on Chouigui, across more than 100 square miles between the two brigade groups. A US Army tank platoon commander in Blade Force (Lieutenant Freeland A. Daubin) later lectured to the US Army's Armor School that Hull's order was 'one of the most quaintly phrased missions ever given any fighting force in the entire history of the profession of arms'. Brigadier General Robinett characterized it as 'the tragedy that occurs when faulty tactics and weak equipment are joined with stout hearts in modern mechanized warfare'.

Robinett was still effectively commanding CCB, while his superior (Major General Lunsford E. Oliver) lagged behind in Algeria until late in the Battle for Tebourba. The CCB had its own problems with training and tactics. The tanks had practised charging the enemy across open terrain, while the armoured infantry had practised dismounting in the hills and trees, without combining arms.

THE FIRST SKIRMISHES IN TUNISIA

On 10–11 November, signals intercepts revealed Kesselring's expectation that the Allies would land from the sea at Bone or Tunis. On 12 November, the British airdropped a battalion of paratroopers on Bone airfield, and landed 6th Commando from the sea, but the Axis air forces were ready to bomb them. The 36th Brigade Group (Northern Group) caught up, then continued along the coast, taking the paras and commandos along. The 36th Brigade Group had formed with three infantry battalions, some 25-pdr guns and a US company of M3 medium tanks. However, they struggled on the coastal road – a journey then of at least 170 miles from Bone through Mateur to the objective: Bizerte. They were still approaching the border on 16 November, when British and US paratroops reached the other side in French vehicles. On 17 November, they met German defenders at Tabarka, about halfway to Bizerte. On 28 November, they were stopped by German paratroops and light armour at Djefna. The shipping of 1st Commando from Tabarka, 60 miles closer to Bizerte, on the night of 30 November to 1 December, made no difference. Indeed, that particular German line held until 3 May 1943.

Most Allied groups travelled into Tunisia overland, via Beja to Medjez el Bab. Medjez, which was 35 miles from Tunis by the quickest highway of the time (south of the river), offered a bridge over the Medjerda River and two highways to Tunis (see map opposite). It was held by about 9,000 men and 15 tanks of the French Army of Tunisia, which had abandoned Tunis rather than cooperate with the Axis. German paratroops followed them and occupied the eastern approaches to the town. After some days of bluff, manoeuvring and negotiation, the confrontation turned deadly on 19 November. By then, the Germans were greatly outnumbered in both troops and firepower, given the arrival of British paratroops and armoured cars and US artillery. Nevertheless, that night the Germans swam across the river and captured the bridge, even though the Allies had prepared it for demolition.

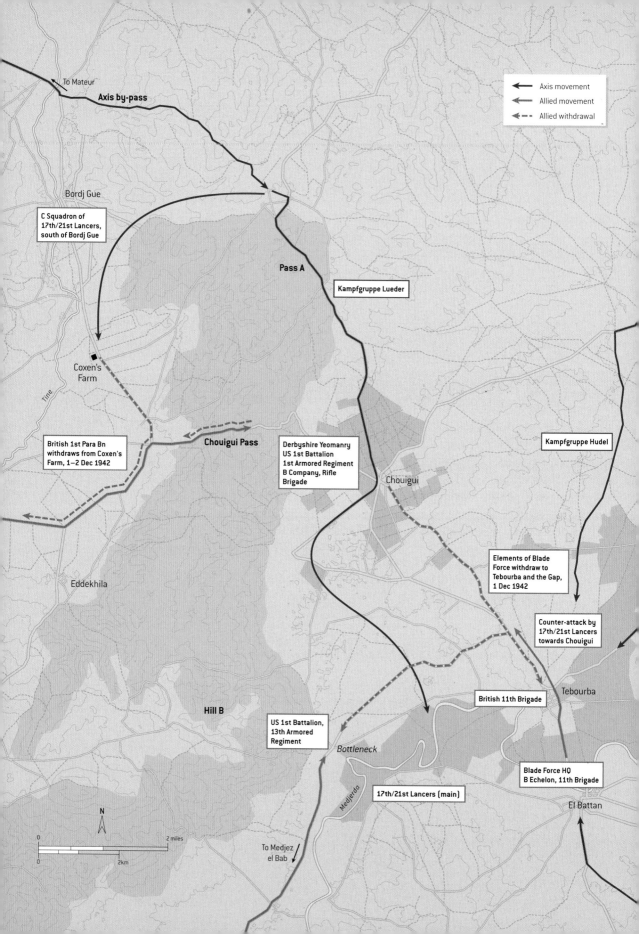

To Mateur

Axis by-pass

Axis movement
Allied movement
Allied withdrawal

Bordj Gue

C Squadron of
17th/21st Lancers,
south of Bordj Gue

Pass A

Kampfgruppe Lueder

Tine

Coxen's
Farm

British 1st Para Bn
withdraws from Coxen's
Farm, 1–2 Dec 1942

Chouigui Pass

Derbyshire Yeomanry
US 1st Battalion
1st Armored Regiment
B Company, Rifle
Brigade

Chouigui

Kampfgruppe Hudel

Eddekhila

Elements of Blade
Force withdraw to
Tebourba and the Gap,
1 Dec 1942

Counter-attack by
17th/21st Lancers
towards Chouigui

Tebourba

Hill B

US 1st Battalion,
13th Armored
Regiment

Bottleneck

British 11th Brigade

Medjerda

Blade Force HQ
B Echelon, 11th Brigade

El Battan

17th/21st Lancers (main)

N

0   2 miles

0   2km

To Medjez
el Bab

Within hours, the Allies abandoned the town and headed towards a ridge about halfway to Beja.

On 24 November, Lieutenant-General Kenneth A.N. Anderson (First Army) ordered Major-General Vyvyan Evelegh (78th Division) to resume the offensive. The southern brigade (11th Brigade Group) attacked Medjez on 25 November. The German 3rd Battalion, 5th Parachute Regiment, abandoned Medjez overnight, after inflicting heavy casualties on the Lancashire Fusiliers. The 11th Brigade Group pushed a Bailey bridge over the demolished span of the stone bridge, and sent the East Surreys over in the evening of 26 November.

The East Surreys reached Tebourba about 1000hrs on 27 November, pushed a patrol onto Point 186 to its east, and captured the bridge at El Bathan to its south. In the afternoon, the Axis counter-attacked from the north-east, but 25-pdrs from a battery of 132nd Field Regiment claimed to knock out ten tanks, for the loss of six of the eight guns. Tebourba was, by current highways, only 22 miles west of Tunis and 45 miles south of Bizerte.

The rest of 11th Brigade Group (part of a US battalion with 25 M3 medium tanks; a company of 12 US tank destroyers; a company of US armoured cars; a platoon of US 75mm self-propelled howitzers; and a US intelligence platoon) caught up that evening.

Nineteen US M3 medium tanks and the 5th Northamptonshire Regiment attacked towards Djedeida at 1300hrs on 28 November, but lost five tanks, probably to the two 88mm guns there. At dusk, their positions were withdrawn to 2,000 yards from Djedeida. Another attack was ordered for 0645hrs, 29 November, but by that time the enemy had been reinforced, and inflicted even more casualties. Nevertheless, First Army HQ told Allied journalists that Djedeida, only 14 miles from Tunis by the highway, across generally open, downhill terrain, was captured and held.

On 25 November, at 0700hrs, Blade Force had started its advance from Beja to Mateur, i.e., between the northern and southern brigade groups. The US element

OPPOSITE
The battlefield around Tebourba, November–December 1942. The hill marked 'B' is where the American film producer Darryl F. Zanuck's photographers were filming the Panzer IIIs to their east.

The Valentine XI's main armament was a 75mm gun, identifiable by its muzzle brake. (RACTM 2792/E/6)

continued eastwards to occupy Chouigui Pass and to raid Djedeida, while the British element took an unfinished road north towards Mateur. The US element defeated two Axis explorations of the highway from Mateur to Chouigui Pass. It concentrated on Chouigui village late on 26 November, presumably to block all possible routes from Mateur to Tebourba.

C Squadron of the 17th/21st Lancers was left at Bordj Gue – 8 miles by the highway north of Chouigui. It faced an Axis force at the next bridge, about 2,700 yards to the north, where a single 88mm gun kept the British tanks at bay. On 28 November, C Squadron observed Panzers supporting workers in the improvement of the track eastwards from the Axis bridge. This track turns southwards through an inferior quality pass, directly north of Chouigui, and less than 9 miles from Tebourba. The track was marked on French and Allied maps, so everybody could realize that the Germans were bypassing Bordj Gue.

Blade Force HQ gave orders at 1300hrs to move after dark to Chouigui, but enemy paratroops were reported in Chouigui Pass, so the move was postponed until daylight. By 1000hrs on 29 November, the British element of Blade Force (except C Squadron of the 17th/21st Lancers) consolidated with the US element. They were attacked by Axis aircraft during the rest of the day. Heavier losses were suffered by the unarmoured echelons, which were operating over dozens of miles, with supply lines stretching hundreds of miles further.

A Valentine III of 4th Troop, C Squadron, 17th/21st Lancers, during a pause for maintenance and mail, probably near Bordj Gue, Tunisia, in late November 1942. (Photo by Sgt. Loughlin/Imperial War Museums via Getty Images)

At night, the British AFVs withdrew 6 miles through Chouigui Pass, while the Americans leaguered in or behind the pass. Before dawn on 30 November, the British AFVs returned to Chouigui, but to more dispersed positions. The Americans extended their positions further east, while the British preferred the vineyards south of Chouigui, where even the tank crews dug trenches. At 0900hrs, Axis artillery opened fire from the hills to the north, before being silenced by 25-pdrs. Thereafter, attacks by Axis aircraft were more numerous than ever. The 17th/21st Lancers lost one Crusader tank, one Valentine tank, one crewman killed and two men wounded to air attacks.

At 1650hrs, Panzers were reported on the road between Djedeida and Tebourba, but the reporter had misplaced the sound of the three Tigers and four Panzer IIIs of the 501st Heavy Tank Battalion, which were coming up the highway from Tunis to Djedeida in time to join the counter-offensive on 1 December. The 17th/21st Lancers sallied south-eastwards, but gave up at dusk (1703hrs). All night they received reports of enemy tanks and infantry moving through Chouigui Pass, as far south as their right flank, i.e., 3 miles north of Tebourba.

COMBAT

PANZERS COUNTER-ATTACK

At 2000hrs on 30 November, the 10th Panzer Division received orders to attack Tebourba at dawn. The Panzers started on 1 December at 0800hrs German time (0600hrs Allied time), allowing 75 minutes before sunrise to take positions before the Allies could see to shoot.

Kampfgruppe *Lüder* (Major Hans-Georg Lüder) came through the more difficult pass with one company from the 190th Panzer Battalion (nominally five Panzer IIs and 12 Panzer IIIs, including a Befehlspanzer III), a battalion of *Panzergrenadiers*, an anti-aircraft platoon (probably two 88mm guns, plus a 20mm cannon) and a platoon of engineers.

Kampfgruppe *Hudel* (Hauptmann Helmut E. Hudel) came from the north-east with two Panzer companies (probably one company held 17 Panzer IIIs, while the other held ten Panzer IVs with long 75mm guns, two Panzer IVs with short 75mm gun/howitzers, and one Befehlspanzer III), one company of eight or nine Marder III 76.2mm self-propelled anti-tank guns, a company of eight or nine 75mm towed guns, and one company of dismounted motorcycle infantry.

Lüder continued to the west of Chouigui, contained Chouigui Pass, and sent part to contain the 'Bottleneck' (the narrowest part of the gap between the river and the mountains, through which the railway line and the highway passed from Medjez to Tebourba). Kampfgruppe *Hudel* passed east of Chouigui towards Tebourba, leaving a Panzer company and some infantry to contain the village. The 10th Panzer Division's commander (Generalleutnant Wolfgang Fischer) was in the frontline, visiting the HQs of each *Kampfgruppe*.

Blade Force's actions remain confusing. C Squadron of the 17th/21st Lancers remained in the night-time harbour west of Chouigui Pass. The rest of the Lancers withdrew at 0630hrs into a new leaguer – an action normally executed after dusk. The new leaguer was in the olive groves along the river, 3 miles west of Tebourba, and about 1,000 yards east of the Bottleneck. Probably Blade Force HQ recalled the Lancers for its own protection. As of 0800hrs on 30 November, Blade Force HQ had moved east of the Bottleneck, on the highway just north of the olive groves. From there, it must have moved into the olive groves, given air attacks and reports of tanks around Djedeida in the evening. Early on 1 December, it must have belatedly decided it needed the Lancers for its own protection.

The HQ and A Company of the US 1st Battalion (Lieutenant Colonel John K. Waters) of 1st Armored Regiment also abandoned Chouigui. They might have lingered in the pass, but at some point during the day consolidated in the Bottleneck. The CCB's other light-tank battalion (the 1st Battalion, under Colonel John H. Todd of 13th Armored Regiment) had reached the Bottleneck the night before, having passed through Medjez.

These strange withdrawals left Chouigui defended by about 30 US light tanks from B Company (Major William R. Tuck) and C Company (Major Rudolph Barlow), ten armoured cars and ten scout cars from the Derbyshire Yeomanry, a motorized infantry company from the Rifle Brigade, eight 6-pdrs and eight 25-pdrs. Captain Edward A. Clarke, the second-in-command of the armoured cars, wrote of being surprised at 0800hrs, even though this was 45 minutes after dawn:

> [We] were surprised to find [our]selves being shelled by 12 Mk. IV tanks approaching from the north through a narrow pass in the hills – a most unexpected line of attack … Panzer IVs appeared from the hills north-east of Chouigui and moved to the south-east under shell-fire from our 25-pounders (which were near to us). We got permission to withdraw the squadron about two miles south-east.

The armoured cars and the US light tanks withdrew through the British infantrymen (B Company, 10th Battalion of the Rifle Brigade), who were horrified to see Panzers deploy from column into V-shape, then take hull-down positions at a range of about 1,500 yards. The company's 2-pdrs, the 6-pdrs of A Battery of 72nd Anti-Tank Regiment, and the US 37mm tank guns probably did not bother to fire at such range. The eight 25-pdrs (C Battery of 12th Royal Horse Artillery) fired directly from behind, however, but without success. Forward observation officers called indirect fire from the 25-pdrs of 132nd Field Regiment, which was in support to the 1st East Surreys at Tebourba. The 3.7in howitzers of 457th Light Battery joined in from near the 17th/21st Lancers' new leaguer.

The Panzers paused, while awaiting an attack by 12 Junkers Ju 87 Stuka dive-bombers. At some point after the dive-bombing, the defenders received permission to withdraw, covered by indirect fire. The 8th Platoon of the Rifle Brigade had been decimated by the dive-bombing. Now most of its personnel were cut off by ground troops. Three of the company's ten Bren Gun Carriers were knocked out while withdrawing to Tebourba.

The rest of Blade Force was squeezed into the olive groves by the Bottleneck – about 4 miles south of Chouigui, 6 miles directly south of the pass through which Lüder had come, and 3 miles west of Tebourba. The railway line ran north-eastwards and perpendicular to Lüder's advance. Clarke's war diary continues:

> By this time, the 17th/21st Lancers, 10th RB, and two guns from 72nd Anti-Tank Regt. were engaging enemy tanks of which we could see about twenty. Col. Hull sent for 1st DY commander immediately the squadron reached the olive grove … There were a good many other troops (infantry, RASC, etc.) in this olive grove which were not under Col. Hull's command.

Ju 87s dive-bombed the position, during which Major John F. Crompton-Inglefield dislocated his shoulder in a collision with a branch, so Clarke took command of the squadron.

VALENTINES COUNTER-ATTACK

At 1000hrs, the Valentines and US light tanks were ordered to counter-attack the positions that the 17th/21st Lancers had departed less than four hours earlier. A and B squadrons and Regimental Headquarters (RHQ) of the 17th/21st Lancers held 24 tanks: 17 Valentines armed with 2-pdr guns (of which three were in unit HQ), five Crusader IIIs (6-pdrs), and two Crusader II close-support tanks (76mm howitzers). Their war diary explains:

> B Squadron were ordered to take up position. On coming on to a bare ridge short of this position, they came into action against enemy tanks which had over-run the infantry guns [towed 2-pdrs]. As soon as B Squadron were in action, RHQ moved up to strengthen their left flank and A Squadron was moved from the olive grove to the high

AT THE FRONT IN NORTH AFRICA

US forces were joined by the American film director John Ford (Field Photographic Section, Office of Strategic Services) and the film producer Darryl F. Zanuck (US Army Signal Corps). As civilians, they had worked for 20th Century Fox. As soldiers, each commanded a few photographers using Bell & Howell 16mm movie cameras with telephoto lenses. Zanuck acquired all footage, then produced a documentary (released in February 1943, by the War Department, titled *At the Front in North Africa*). Both Ford and Zanuck were using Technicolor film, which is brilliant in colour but fuzzy in definition.

The first of these two still images (below left) is looking from the south-eastern corner of Djebel el Aroussia (Hill 'B' on the map on page 56). The slope reaches to 259m (1,850ft) at its nearest summit. The camera is looking eastwards. The highest ground on the horizon (more than 5 miles away) is Djebel Maiana. It was marked on all current maps with a summit of 186m (610ft), although today it has been denuded by quarrying. Tebourba is seen at its foot as a white area, running thinly from left to right. The concrete highway from Medjez appears from the bottom-right corner of the frame, and runs north-eastwards between the two areas of smoke and off frame to the left. A track crosses the road at bottom right. Off frame to the right, it crosses the railway line and continues through olive groves to the nearest bend of the river. The river appears about halfway up the right edge of the frame.

It appears as the lower boundary of a darker vegetated area and continues from right to left, below the white area of Tebourba, before (invisible in this image) it curves right, around the west and south of Tebourba, through El Bathan, behind Djebel Maiana and on towards Djedeida. The single-track railway takes a straight line behind the white smoke to re-join the concrete road just off the left of the frame. About equidistant between the two areas of smoke are some haystacks, on the north side of the highway. Over the top of the haystacks is a track running almost up the centre-line of the frame. Subsequent footage suggests that this track would be the southern limit of the German advance on 1 December.

In the second of these still images (below right), the photographer has zoomed in on the track (which is most apparent above the middle haystack) along which Panzer 3Js and 3Ls are firing southwards. The haystacks are only 600 yards from the nearest bend of the river. The tanks are firing at parts of 11th Brigade and Blade Force in the olive groves between the railway line and the river. The narrator claims that five Panzers came into view (Panzer IIIs were organized five to a platoon), while another five were obscured by the rise below the frame. Meanwhile, indirect fire is closing in. Subsequent footage shows the Panzers wheeling leftwards and northwards, revealing bright red Nazi flags on their rears as recognition signals to aircraft.

ground some 1,500 yards south and in rear of B Squadron's position. B Squadron's position was on a bare ridge, whilst the enemy were in trees and vineyards [2,000 yards away] which was a disadvantage to the regiment whose guns were mainly 2-pounders. The enemy evidently had watched us for days from the hills and knew our gun positions exactly. The nature of the country was such that a hull-down tank was visible for at least 2,000 yards, at which range the enemy engaged us and managed to knock out five Crusaders.

The RHQ took up positions to the left of B Squadron. One Valentine (Major Nigel Dugdale, the unit's second-in-command) claimed to knock out two or three Panzers. Dugdale was followed by the intelligence officer (Lieutenant Bliss), who was manning the rear-link radio:

> Just in front of me Nigel Dugdale is blazing away with his two-pounder, but I'm damned if I can spot his target. We'll go and have a better look.
>
> 'Driver advance.' The whole tank shudders and a red flame seems to shoot out from the front. For a moment I think my gunner has started firing without orders, and I curse him through the intercom.
>
> 'We've been hit, Sir' – it's the driver's voice in my 'phones.
>
> 'OK, can you reverse? – get turret down – halt.'
>
> At the same time, Nigel's tank is hit [on the turret ring: it knocked out the driver (Lance-Corporal Dawson), jammed the turret, and jammed the transmission] and three figures bale out of the turret [Dugdale, Lance-Corporal Sollis and Trooper Flanagan, all wounded slightly]. They climb on the front of the tank, evidently trying to extricate the driver. Some HE comes down, and all three are blown off the tank, but they're up and have another go.

After the three men were blown off a second time, they hid for an hour until the battlefield seemed quiet, then made a third attempt, when more HE fire blew them off the tank, killing Flanagan and wounding Dugdale in the face, arm and hand. Bliss watched Dugdale and Sollis bend over Flanagan, then come running back. Blood was

A Panzer 3J armed with a 50mm L42 gun and assigned to the 10th Panzer Division faces south-eastwards on the main street in Tebourba, as prisoners from the Hampshire Regiment are escorted to the railway station, in the afternoon of 4 December 1942. (ullstein bild via Getty Images)

streaming down Dugdale's face. Bliss reached for his first-aid box, while Dugdale reported events. Bliss could see his commander's Valentine on the left, and endeavoured to join him, in order to maintain the radio link between RHQ and Blade Force HQ. Far to the left, out of range of his 2-pdr, he could see some Panzers advancing in column. The war diary continues:

> The Regiment at this time was on the left of Blade Force, with B Squadron on the right of the Regiment and the left flank covered by RHQ. A Squadron was in reserve one mile south-west; 24 tanks were seen to be moving around our left flank to the west. Bliss radioed to his unit commander (Lieutenant-Colonel Richard G. Hamilton-Russell), asking for any messages to be relayed to Colonel Hull:
>
> 'Yes', his voice comes back slowly and clearly, 'Inform "sunray" [default code-word for commander] I seem to be outflanked and out-numbered. I intend to fight a delaying action, if possible hold them off till dusk.'
>
> Air activity is increasing now, and we return gradually from ridge to ridge [towards Tebourba].

The Lancers lost six Valentines and two Crusaders. The British blamed the US 1st Battalion of 13th Armoured Regiment for the German advance on the gap, but that unit left no explanation of its own. Todd would be killed within weeks. He may not have been around on the day. Todd's battalion held only two companies of light tanks throughout the fighting for Tebourba, while its third company was developing a French armoured force in Oran. B and C companies of 1st Battalion, 1st Armored Regiment, could have joined Todd, but perhaps were still in flight from Chouigui.

THE BATTLE FOR THE 'BOTTLENECK'

Colonel Hull had stayed in the olive grove with the transport and the Derbyshire Yeomanry's armoured cars. The only source for this part of the battle is Clarke:

> Suddenly a further 20 tanks – German tanks – which should have been engaged by the American Honeys [M3 Lights] were seen moving due east towards us, well to the south of the 17th/21st Lancers position and without anyone to stop them. Col. Hull then ordered Capt. Clarke to put all the armoured cars he could on the forward edge of the olive grove to impose maximum delay and allow soft vehicles in the grove to withdraw towards Le Jez [Medjez].

Most of the other armoured cars escorted the soft vehicles back to Medjez, which seemed simple enough until they came under small-arms fire from about 100 paratroops in the hills, about 1.3 miles south-west of the Bottleneck. The 5th Troop (Lieutenant Cliff Jones) defended the Bottleneck, with the standard inventory of one Daimler armoured car (coaxial 2-pdr and machine gun), one Humber armoured car (coaxial 15mm and 7.92mm machine guns) and two scout cars. The 4th Troop went to the south-east corner, where the olive groves meet the river. Clarke and the rear-link officer (Lieutenant Dennis Ospalak) stayed in their armoured cars to oversee everything. The armoured cars of 5th Troop opened fire at 400 yards:

> They were barely in position when the tanks opened up, and in a few minutes there was pandemonium. The savage long-barrelled 75s on the Mk. IVs were firing flat out. AP shells whistled past our armoured cars, and HE bursting among the retreating transport showed that it had also been spotted. Our two-pounders replied and a solitary mountain gun [presumably a 3.7in howitzer of 457th Light Battery] which chanced to be in the olive grove joined the unequal contest on our side, firing over open sights. Soon Cliff Jones's Daimler motored out of action, and as he approached I saw a large jagged hole in the hull. He stopped and asked if he could withdraw as his gunner, [Trooper D.O.L.] Laming, was badly wounded [and would die the next day].

This Panzer 3N was knocked out by British 6-pdr guns while following Tiger 231 of the 2nd Company, 501st Heavy Tank Battalion, on the road to Robaa, Tunisia, 31 January 1943. (RACTM 1070/B/4)

Sergeant W.W. Youngman was left in charge of 5th Troop, while Clarke and Ospalak acted as the links between the forward troops and the withdrawal:

> When the olive grove was nearly clear of transport I told the remaining cars out in front to withdraw and heard the heartening news that three enemy tanks were blazing.

Hartmann (Lüder's ordnance officer) remembered that the fighting was as close as 10m (11 yards), and resulted in the loss of eight Panzer IIIs and IVs, 11 dead, 16 wounded and four missing.

VALENTINES DEFEND TEBOURBA

Most Allies were around Tebourba. Increasingly, they relied on artillery. The British deployed 74 field guns around Tebourba, most of them close to the front so as to double as anti-tank guns. Sixteen 155mm howitzers of US 5th Field Artillery Battalion had set up south-east of Tebourba overnight 28/29 November, although without ammunition. At some point, six 105mm self-propelled howitzers from 27th Armored Field Artillery Battalion deployed in the gap, halfway to Medjez. The battalion's other three batteries were in transit, as was 175th Field Artillery Battalion (towed 105mm howitzers).

At 1130hrs, the 17th/21st Lancers were ordered to join 11th Brigade Group's line before Tebourba, but, according to their war diarist, 'one of the chief difficulties in Tebourba was the fact that there was no commander there and therefore no co-ordination of the defence'. This is a clear criticism of Brigadier Edward E. Cass, who stayed to the west of the Bottleneck. At one point, the Germans got as close as 500 yards from 11th Brigade HQ. Robinett was most critical:

> The methods and means employed by Cass to co-ordinate such a heterogenous force are not known. But American and British equipment and procedures were quite different. It is, therefore, extremely doubtful that there was any effective co-ordination within Cass' command … If to the uncertainty resulting from faulty command arrangements are added the mistakes of beginners, it is no wonder that confusion was so prevalent.

The remnants of Blade Force's infantry (B Company, Rifle Brigade) joined 11th Brigade's forward line, until they were overrun by enemy infantry. The 8th Platoon was of little use after its casualties at Chouigui, so the 6th Platoon formed the rearguard. Lieutenant (Alexander) James Wilson was commanding:

> The riflemen as usual reacted superbly when it came to quick movement: soon we were all in the dead ground behind our ridge, jumping on our trucks like a load of football supporters leaving a lost match. Thank God, too. I had remembered my training: the trucks were parked facing the exit, so we could drive straight out of our area and on to the Tebourba road. We bumped agonisingly over the rough field between us and the tarmac, followed by our anti-tank guns. Once on the firm surface, Rifleman Gough and the others put their feet down. It had been a near thing. As we drove into Tebourba we passed a 5.5-inch medium gun [probably a US 155mm howitzer], sighted to fire down the road in an anti-tank role.

B Company lost two officers and 45 other ranks. It was sent to the rear until late December.

The 11th Brigade's infantry settled somewhere south of the junction between the highway to Mateur and the highway to Medjez – just 1,000 yards outside of Tebourba by some accounts. The 17th/21st Lancers eventually (by 1310hrs) formed a new line about 2,400 yards north-west of the outer limits of Tebourba, behind a peak marked as 82m (269ft) on the current map.

The 17th/21st Lancers were left with 11 Valentines and five Crusaders. They could have recalled their C Squadron, which was blocking the highway at Bordj Gue (see map on page 56). By noon, C Squadron was supporting 1st Parachute Regiment in the defence of Coxen's Farm from German infantry that had occupied the hills above. Eventually, the paras and Valentines advanced northwards from Bordj Gue to cut Axis communications between Mateur and Chouigui. However, the attack did not commence until 1600hrs and failed. The farm was evacuated. In retrospect, C Squadron would have been more useful at Tebourba.

Axis forces lined up 2 miles to the north-west of A and B squadrons. The Panzers were under orders not to take needless risks, given their overall numerical inferiority. The 17th/21st Lancers reported their constant threats as dive-bombers. They were unaware that German infantry and Panzers were infiltrating the olive groves near the Bottleneck. At some point, somebody used the rear-link radio net to warn Blade Force HQ, 'Are you aware that there are 20 tanks approaching your location?' A battery of eight 25-pdrs was nearest the HQ: it claimed to knock out some tanks and drive the rest away. At 1320hrs, Blade Force HQ fled south-westwards for 2 miles through the Bottleneck. Hull had no deputy, so his last message placed Hamilton-Russell in command of Blade Force.

PANZER IIIS AND TIGERS

Around the time the 17th/21st Lancers formed their new line, Kampfgruppe Djedeida engaged British infantry in the woods between Djedeida and Tebourba. Soon, the Lancers could see – 6 miles to their west, and north of the woods – US M3 medium tanks (2nd Battalion, 13th Armored Regiment) open fire from olive groves. Unknown to the Lancers, the Americans were firing on the three Tigers and four Panzer IIIs (likely all Panzer 3Ns) of the 501st Heavy Tank Battalion, 2,000m (2,200 yards) away. The M3s advanced, the Panzers withdrew; the M3s chased, but seven were knocked out by German anti-tank guns. The Tigers advanced and knocked out two more M3s in the olive groves, at 150m (164 yards).

However, the Tigers had reached their limit for the day. Leutnant Eberhard Deichmann dismounted his Tiger to get a better view, and was mortally wounded by a rifle shot in his stomach. Another Tiger's engine overheated when the air vents became blocked with vegetation. A Panzer 3N closed up to protect it. German infantry arrived to consolidate, before the other two Tigers and three Panzer IIIs withdrew.

THE FINAL BATTLES OF THE FIRST DAY

The other two *Kampfgruppen* took advantage of Kampfgruppe Djedeida's attack by advancing south-eastwards towards Tebourba. The 11th Brigade contracted further on the northern outskirts of Tebourba. By 1700hrs, most of Blade Force withdrew south of Tebourba along the 2 miles of road towards the bridge at El Bathan. The 5th Northamptonshire Regiment took up positions astride the road immediately south of Tebourba; the 17th/21st Lancers were to the east of the road; and the 1st East Surreys were defending the bridge.

That evening, a patrol of Northamptonshires spotted 27 Panzers leaguered in trees less than a mile away. The Northamptonshires and the East Surreys received orders that night to withdraw. The Hampshires (in the woods towards Djedeida) did not.

THE SECOND DAY

The two northern *Kampfgruppen* were just 1,000m (1,100 yards) from Tebourba by the start of the second day. They aimed merely to prevent the defenders re-connecting with their comrades in the Bottleneck. Part of 11th Brigade Group remained in Tebourba itself, but the bulk seems to have stayed to its south, up to El

OVERLEAF

The Battle for Tebourba, Tunisia, 1 December 1942.

Bathan bridge. The 17 Valentines and Crusaders (a replacement Crusader III had arrived overnight) were distributed amongst the infantry as anti-tank support. Tankless crewmen, armed with sub-machine guns and Bren light machine guns from the tanks, joined the infantry. The 17th/21st Lancers HQ held three Valentines, four scout cars and six Bren Gun Carriers; A Squadron held five Valentines and a close-support Crusader II; B Squadron had three Valentines, four Crusader IIIs and a close-support Crusader II.

Allied artillery had been resupplied and reinforced, although the US 155mm howitzers departed without permission, after failing to receive ammunition in the night.

At El Bathan bridge, the East Surreys received machine-gun and mortar fire from German paratroops on slightly higher ground, about 1,000 yards to the south. On three occasions, the East Surreys perceived the Germans as building up to an attack, and requested tanks. On the first occasion, A Squadron sent three Valentines across the bridge, but they were repelled by anti-tank rifle bullets. They were led by Lieutenant Hawkins, whose driver suddenly exclaimed, 'Excuse me, sir, but they are coming through the front.' All three tanks returned, only for two to be abandoned (one with a punctured radiator, the other with damaged steering). The 10th Panzer Division later put at least one of these Valentines (named 'Apple Sammy') back into service, and would use it to lead an attack against its original users near Kasserine Pass on 21 February 1943.

Captain Michael C. Watson of B Squadron commanded the next two sweeps, supported by the two 76mm howitzers on the Crusader II close-support tanks of B Squadron's HQ. The German paratroops infiltrated through the olive groves, and sniped into the perimeter. This fire pacified Blade Force.

Both the Allies and the Germans were focused on the Bottleneck. No British tanks were there, although more British infantry and US tanks and armoured infantry had arrived overnight. The British units in the Tebourba Gap were receiving orders and information direct from 78th Division HQ. Whatever Hull and Cass did that day is not recorded in any war diaries, not even their own. Hull must have stayed in a gulley west of the Bottleneck, and more than 5 miles from El Bathan. Overnight, the Americans had withdrawn from his command in favour of CCB HQ. Nevertheless, the Americans wasted their tanks in an ill-coordinated counter-attack out of the Bottleneck straight into the German anti-tank guns. The crews of the Panzer IIIs prepared to counter-attack, although most do not seem to have bothered, as the Americans abandoned their efforts.

Meanwhile, Kampfgruppe Djedeida tried to reach Tebourba via the wooded highway. After losing one Panzer III burnt out, and another two disabled, the remaining Tiger and two Panzer IIIs switched to the road north of the woods in time to participate in the rout of the US tanks, at around 1100hrs.

At 1900hrs, the 17th/21st Lancers' wheeled vehicles withdrew, followed by the tanks. The 1st East Surreys were the last unit of Blade Force to cross the bridge at El Bathan, before engineers blew it up. The withdrawal from El Bathan was southwards to meet the highway from Tunis, then westwards through Medjez to Oued Zarga – a drive of about 40 miles. Without lights, and with other traffic, it took more than five hours.

STATISTICS AND ANALYSIS

OUTCOMES: MATERIAL

On 1 December, the Allies lost 17 tanks (eight British; nine US) around Tebourba, while the Germans lost perhaps 12. Evelegh told journalists that the Germans had lost 45 Panzers, of 60 in the country, but his absurdity was proven the next day, when the same HQ estimated 45 Panzers attacking.

On 2 December, the 17th/21st Lancers lost at least another two Valentines in defending El Bathan bridge, while the Americans lost more than 30 tanks in a counter-attack. The German communiqué claimed 34 tanks, six armoured cars and 200 prisoners for that day alone. First Army estimated about 40 Allied tanks lost up to the evening of 2 December. Only one Panzer III was written off that day; another two were disabled.

The Germans captured Tebourba on 3 December. Only 200 of more than 700 Hampshires escaped. Just two Panzer IIIs and one Tiger were involved in that fight. The bulk of the Panzer IIIs launched a diversionary attack against the Bottleneck, while German infantry infiltrated across the high ground on either side.

Axis forces spent 4 December consolidating Tebourba, investigating the many abandoned weapons, rounding up Allied prisoners and their own missing personnel, maintaining their equipment, and preparing for the next phase.

The 10th Panzer Division estimated that from 1–4 December it knocked out or captured 55 tanks, four armoured cars, 300 other automobiles, four anti-tank guns,

This Valentine III, named 'Apple Sammy', was abandoned by A Squadron, 17th/21st Lancers, at Tebourba on 3 December 1942. The 7th Panzer Regiment, 10th Panzer Division, painted its symbol (a bison) on the turret sides. On 21 February 1943, it used 'Apple Sammy' to lead a column of Panzer IIIs and IVs into the night-time leaguer of 26th Armoured Brigade, which was defending the road from Kasserine Pass to Thala. After fighting at point-blank range, the Germans withdrew, with remarkably few casualties on either side. (IWM NA 844)

six 155mm and six 105mm howitzers, 13 smaller artillery pieces (probably US 75mm guns, British 88mm 25-pdrs and British 3.7in or 94mm pack howitzers), 40 mortars, 38 machine guns and 1,000–1,100 prisoners. On 5 December, Nehring's communiqué reported that after mopping up Tebourba, the cumulative haul of prisoners surpassed 1,100, captured artillery passed 40 pieces, and the count of destroyed tanks passed 70. The British admitted the loss of 53 of their 74 field guns around Tebourba. The Allies claimed 36 Panzers in the same period – around double the true number.

Eisenhower drafted a long report that he telegrammed early on 5 December to his Chief of Staff in London, with instructions to forward it to a frustrated Prime Minister Churchill. However, despite many words and pages, Eisenhower danced around the issues. The following is his most substantive comment: 'the counter-attacks of 1 to 3 December set us back considerably and caused us material losses'.

The German attacks towards Medjez reached their zenith on 10 December, just short of the town, both north and south of the river – and there the frontlines stuck until April 1943.

By 11 December, the CCB had lost 50 medium tanks, 84 light tanks, 15 105mm self-propelled howitzers, 22 75mm self-propelled guns, 232 other half-tracks, 66 2½-ton trucks and 72 1-ton trailers. The CCB was rendered ineffective until mid-January:

it represented half the strength of the US 1st Armored Division (the other half remained in Britain).

The British lost 25 Valentines and 15 Crusaders. The 17th/21st Lancers were left with just 11 Valentines and six Crusaders, despite replacements and consolidation. The British had contributed fewer tanks than the Americans, so lost fewer tanks. They had contributed most of the other arms to the three brigade groups, so they lost the most wheeled vehicles.

The total loss of Allied tanks was 174. The Germans underestimated 134 Allied tanks knocked out. For the period 1–10 December, the Axis claimed to have shot down 79 Allied planes over Tunisia, and another 112 over the Mediterranean thereabouts.

OUTCOMES: COMMANDERS

Eisenhower was depressed and guilty at his failure to capture Tunisia within weeks of the landings in Algeria. As the campaign dragged through the cold, wet winter, he often thought about resigning, but hung on, and commanded the expeditions to Sicily, mainland Italy, France and onwards to Germany.

Eisenhower privately blamed Anderson's caution. Anderson blamed the French who aided the Germans. Eisenhower later detached the French Army of Tunisia and the US Corps from First Army. Anderson's command was dissolved after the campaign. He returned to Britain to take over Second Army, which was preparing to invade France; but once General Bernard L. Montgomery returned, after commanding Eighth Army from Tunisia to Italy, Anderson was demoted to Britain's Eastern Command (which Anderson had held before First Army).

Evelegh retained command of 78th Division until December 1943, when he and the commander of 6th Armoured Division were ordered, ridiculously, to switch positions. Less than a year later, after the division's poor performance, he was kicked up and out to the General Staff in London.

Cass retained 11th Brigade until October 1943, when he returned to Britain from Italy to take command of 8th Brigade, 3rd Division. This division was allocated a leading role in the invasion of Normandy in June 1944. He commanded the division for ten days that month after its commander was wounded, but returned to the brigade echelon for the rest of the war.

Hull blamed dive-bombers for Blade Force's failure. The official historian for the 17th/21st Lancers praised Hull's 'superb organization and command of the force', but he was never in a position to see Hull in action (he was commander of C Squadron at the time). Clarke (B Squadron, Derbyshire Yeomanry) wrote:

As it was, Blade's achievements were by no means negligible and it was a very pleasant party. We all had the greatest admiration for Colonel Hull as the commander, and the 17th/21st Lancers, as parent regiment, were most helpful in every way. For B Squadron it was a valuable battle inoculation in which our tasks were very varied and the penalties for errors were not high.

Gordon Highlanders ride the leading Valentine II of 23rd Armoured Brigade into Tripoli, Libya, on 23 January 1943. (IWM E21592)

Blade Force was dissolved around 11 December, when Hull became second-in-command of 26th Armoured Brigade. On 15 January, Anderson handed him the Distinguished Service Order for his actions at Tebourba. Three different men commanded 26th Armoured Brigade during the campaign in Tunisia, after which it was given to Hull. A few months later, he was recalled to the Staff Duties branch in the War Office. As a staff officer, he restored his career, ending up as Chief of the Imperial General Staff.

On 8 January, Robinett was ordered to command a combined-arms force, including his own HQ, as an effective Combat Command HQ. The commander of CCB (Major General Lunsford E. Oliver) was not notified in advance of this change, although he was notified of his return to the United States to command 5th Armored Division. Gradually, most of CCB transferred to Robinett's new command. The 5th Armored Division would deploy to France in July 1944.

In Berlin, Nehring was not treated as the victor. Hitler was displeased with his failure to capture Medjez. Adhering to prior plans, Generaloberst Hans-Jürgen von Arnim arrived on 8 December to establish 5th Panzer Army HQ, which absorbed Nehring's HQ. Nehring remained in Tunis for some days thereafter to help with the transition. In 1943, he took command of a Panzerkorps on the Eastern Front, and finished the war in charge of a Panzerarmee.

Fischer remained in command of the 10th Panzer Division, but was killed on 1 February 1943, when his staff car strayed into an unmarked Italian minefield.

FORCE EMPLOYMENT

Publicly, Eisenhower blamed Allied 'weakness' on the ground and in the air, and the weather, even though the Allies had been preponderant throughout and would not see bad weather until after they lost Tebourba.

A British journalist (Alexander G. Clifford) at Allied Forces HQ reported 'the meagreness of the forces employed' compared to 'massive reinforcements' from Italy and Germany. Another (Philip Jordan) was persuaded by 78th Division HQ every day since 3 December that the Allies were materially inferior. Nevertheless, he publicly blamed Evelegh's over-optimism too.

David Divine, the only non-American journalist embedded with CCB, reported that 'even this new accretion of strength could not overcome the increasing strength of the defences, and the attackers lacked always infantry to consolidate the gains the tanks had made'. On the other hand, he acknowledged CCB's many 'faults':

> From observation I would say that the greatest of them were an initial lack of appreciation of the possibilities of the enemy; a certain indiscipline of the mind; a tendency towards exaggeration … Units behaved as units, and when they were in danger of being overrun showed a tendency to withdraw without reference to the position of the units on either flank, without reference to their responsibility.

Robinett blamed every higher commander.

> The Allies had reached Tunisia too late, with too little, without a balanced force and proper command arrangements, and failed to employ available forces so that they were mutually supporting. But the greater folly was the intermingling of the force of three nations in the same sector.

Robinett was the main source for the US official historian, who wrote:

> The situation on the morning of 2 December called for a well co-ordinated employment of these troops in tactics adapted to certain advantages held by each side … The Allies had larger numbers of tanks and anti-tank guns, and could also count on well-placed artillery, aided by superb observation … Instead of taking advantage of this situation, the Allies frittered away some of their armoured strength in an attempt to pit tanks against tanks without even seeking to benefit from greater numbers.

The British official historian practically ignored the Battle of Tebourba, as has every secondary historian.

At 2315hrs on 20 March 1943, the 9th Battalion, Durham Light Infantry (DLI), 50th Division, advanced over the Wadi Zigzaou to the strongpoint of Ksiba Ouest, while 8th DLI advanced to Ouerzi – 1 mile to the west (left), in the Mareth Line, Tunisia. In between, Royal Engineers blew passes in the Wadi, for the 50th RTR, 23rd Armoured Brigade. The leading Valentine II drowned in 3ft of water. Alongside, Royal Engineers constructed a causeway with fascines and earth, which four Valentines crossed before the fourth tank got stuck in the far pass. At first light, the following Valentines were ordered to return to their assembly area. From 2330hrs, 5th East Yorkshires advanced to the right of Ksiba Ouest, 9th DLI expanded its lodgment, 6th DLI advanced to strongpoints behind Ouerzi, and 42 Valentines crossed an improved causeway before it collapsed. At 0145hrs on 22 March, about 30 Panzer IIIs and IVs of the 15th Panzer Division attacked. Before dawn on 23 March, 50th Division completed its withdrawal. The 50th RTR retained 18 of its 51 Valentines. (IWM NA 1348)

AFTERMATH

In December 1942, Middle East Command's highest authority for the Royal Armoured Corps reported the Valentine as 'definitely obsolete' because of insufficient armour and armament, even with the 6-pdr gun. Independently, Middle East Command's technical authority reported:

> Valentine is an extremely dependable tank and mechanically superior to either Grant or Sherman petrol-engine tanks. As a fighting proposition it falls between two stools, being neither fast enough for a cruiser nor sufficiently well armoured for an assault tank. Of the two roles, the latter is the more suitable, as it is less likely to involve a conflict with enemy AFV, in which the tank has neither the striking power to make a stand nor the speed to get away.

By March 1943, the British First Army in northern Tunisia held two brigades of Churchill tanks, the latest of which carried the 6-pdr gun, a coaxial machine gun, and a third crewman in the turret, and were better protected. These took the lead in subsequent assaults. Valentines were retired from First Army, but stayed in service with the Free French and the British Eighth Army to the south.

A few Valentine IXs reached Eighth Army in late January 1943, although none went into action until 21 March 1943, during the assault on the Mareth Line, on the Tunisian border with Libya. Their 57mm 6-pdr guns matched the 50mm L60 guns on the counter-attacking Panzer 3J Lang and later types, but they accommodated only two men in the turret, and no machine guns.

Moreover, the 6-pdr was useless against fortifications, as HE ammunition had not quite reached the frontlines. For this reason, Middle East Command's technical authority reported that the Valentine IXs 'also failed to find favour owing to their deficiency in fire power. From the point of view of reliability they were every bit as good as Sherman, and though less well protected in front, they had better side armour.'

Victory in North Africa was completed in May 1943. In June 1943, the War Office deleted Valentines from expeditionary forces in Europe, although many remained in French, Soviet, Australian, New Zealand, Indian and British Home Forces. Valentine XIs (75mm gun) were issued to the commanders of anti-tank battalions and batteries in North-West Europe and Italy from late 1944. Some of these units used the 17-pdr self-propelled anti-tank gun (Archer) on the Valentine platform, which had replaced the Valentine in production.

This is the first Panzer 3L to reach Britain, in spring 1943. (RACTM 2896/E/4)

The Valentine was used as the platform for more variants than any other British tank, including an amphibious DD (Duplex Drive), bridge-layers, flails, flamethrowers, the 25-pdr self-propelled field gun (Bishop), artillery observation vehicles (main armament removed), and tractors. None of these was as numerous or useful as the German assault gun on the Panzer III platform, mounting either a long 75mm gun (StuG III) or a 105mm howitzer (StuH III). More StuG IIIs were delivered than Panzer III or Valentine tanks.

The Panzer III remained in service in Europe throughout the war, so continued to duel the Valentine platform, although the inventory was dwindling. Thirty are known to have served in Normandy between June and August 1944. Others were in Italy at the time, and with garrisons in Scandinavia and the Balkans, from where some might have been transferred to active fronts. By then, the duel was likeliest on the Eastern Front, where second-rate Soviet units used Valentine IXs and Xs until the end of the war. Panzer IIIs and Valentines had been fighting for three-and-a-half years – a remarkable record for two pre-war designs in a war of rapid development.

This Valentine XI is serving in North-West Europe as the command tank for a battalion of M10 tank destroyers. (RACTM 0081/C/4)

BIBLIOGRAPHY

Bürker, Ulrich, *Commitment of the 10th Panzer Division in Tunisia* (United States Army Europe HQ, Historical Division, D-174, 1947).

Daniell, David Scott, *Regimental History: The Royal Hampshire Regiment, Volume III, 1918–1954* (Aldershot: Gale & Polden, 1955).

Divine, Arthur Durham, *The Road to Tunis* (London: Collins, 1944).

Eisenhower, Dwight D., *Crusade in Europe* (New York, NY: Doubleday, 1948).

ffrench Blake, R.L.V., *A History of the 17th/21st Lancers, 1922–1959* (London: Macmillan, 1962).

Ford, Ken, *Mailed Fist: 6th Armoured Division at War, 1940–1945* (Thrupp: Sutton Publishing, 2005).

Harris, Mark, *Five Came Back: A Story of Hollywood at War* (New York, NY: Penguin, 2014).

Hastings, R.H.W.S., *The Rifle Brigade in the Second World War, 1939–1945* (Aldershot: Gale & Polden, 1950).

Howe, George F., *The Battle History of the 1st Armored Division* (Nashville, TN: The Battery Press, 1954).

—, *Northwest Africa: Seizing the Initiative in the West* (Washington, DC: Office of the Chief of Military History, Department of the Army, 1957).

Jervois, W.J., *The History of the Northamptonshire Regiment, 1934–1948* (London: The Regimental History Committee, 1953).

Jordan, Philip, *Jordan's Tunis Diary* (London: Collins, 1943).

Macksey, Kenneth, *The Tanks: The History of the Royal Tank Regiment, 1945–1975* (London: Arms & Armour, 1979).

—, *A History of the Royal Armoured Corps and its Predecessors, 1914–1975* (Beaminster: Newtown Publications, 1983).

McBride, Joseph, *Searching for John Ford* (Jackson, MS: University Press of Mississippi, 2011).

Nehring, Walter, *The First Phase of the Engagements in Tunisia up to the Assumption of Command by the Newly Activated 5th Panzer Army Command on 9 December 1942* (United States Army Europe HQ, Historical Division, Foreign Military Studies Branch, D-086, 1947).

—, *The First Phase of the Battle in Tunisia… Part 2* (United States Army Europe HQ, Historical Division, D-147, 1947).

—, *The Development of the Situation in North Africa* (United States Army Europe HQ, Historical Division, D-120, 1947).

Newsome, Bruce Oliver, *Valentine Infantry Tank 1938–45* (Oxford: Osprey, 2016).

—, *The Tiger Tank and Allied Intelligence, Volume I, From Grosstraktor to Tiger 231* (Coronado, CA: Tank Archives Press, 2020).

—, *The Rise and Fall of Western Tanks 1855–1939* (Coronado, CA: Tank Archives Press, 2021).

—, *The Rise and Fall of Western Tanks 1939–1955* (Coronado, CA: Tank Archives Press, 2021).

Perrett, Bryan, *The Valentine in North Africa 1942–43* (London: Ian Allan, 1972).

Playfair, Ian S.O., *The Mediterranean and Middle East, Volume IV, The Destruction of the Axis Forces in Africa* (London: Her Majesty's Stationery Office, 1966).

Robinett, Paul McDonald, *Armor Command* (Washington, DC: United States Armor Association, 1958).

Spielberger, Walter J., *Panzer III and Its Variants* (Atglen, PA: Schiffer, 1993).

United States Military Academy, *The War in North Africa, Part 2, The Allied Invasion* (West Point, NY: 1947).

Zanuck, Darryl F., *Tunis Expedition* (New York, NY: Random House, 1943).

INDEX